# Grow Rich Selling Magazine Ads

Peter E. Ebner

First Edition 2009

Published by
**Peter Ebner Inc**
9251-8 Yonge Street, Suite 144
Richmond Hill, Ontario, L4C 9T3
www.SellingMagazineAds.com

**Canadian Cataloging in Publication Data**

Ebner, Peter 1952-
Grow Rich Selling Magazine Ads

ISBN 978-0-9737011-2-8

1. Selling – Handbooks, manuals, etc.
I. Peter E. Ebner
II. Title: Grow Rich Selling Magazine Ads



Cover design by Valerie Prussak, 2genesis@sympatico.ca

Printed and bound in Canada by
WEBCOM, Toronto, Ontario

# Table of Contents

# Introduction

The days when you could sell magazine ads by calling on a prospect, hand him a media kit and show him that your publication reaches thousands of potential customers at a low CPM are dead and gone. Today's decision makers are more sophisticated, they have a better understanding of their target market and they have more marketing options to consider. Where at one time radio, direct mail, trade shows and magazines were the primary marketing tools more and more decision makers are weighing the benefits of using low cost email campaigns and web marketing to drive their sales, generate leads and improve branding.

While many publications are already feeling the pinch of shrinking magazine advertising dollars, the decline in magazine advertising can, for the most part, be attributed to poor, outdated selling skills.

*Grow Rich Selling Magazine Ads* is a comprehensive field guide that details the strategies and techniques the North America's most successful magazine ad salespeople are using to grow their sales in today's competitive marketplace.

Peter E. Ebner

# Your clients only want to deal with Mr. Ricc

**R**eader **I**ndustry **C**lient **C**ompetition

# R Reader profile

## Understand your publication's unique reader profile

If you don't know your readers, you can't sell magazine ads and I'm not talking about cursory knowledge. You need an in-depth understanding of who your readers are, how they act and what they're thinking, because only then can you show the client that there is a perfect fit between his marketing objectives and your publication.

Every publication has a unique reader profile and for the most part reader profile is determined by editorial content. For example, 2 trade publications that have the same circulation and are distributed to the same target market may attract vastly different readers. Publication "A's" editorial content is directed at upper management while publication "B" focuses on production, which means that even though they have the identical distribution, they are being read by different individuals and therefore will appeal to different advertisers.

While most ad salespeople try to fit the client's products and services to their book, the industry's most successful salespeople take the opposite approach. When looking for new business, they start by understanding what makes their readers unique, then they find clients that have the products and services that their unique readers are looking for.

Here are just some of the questions you must be able to answer.

Who are the primary readers?
Who are the pass-along readers?
Why are they reading your magazine?
What buying decisions can your unique readers make?
What buying influence do your unique readers have?
What spending power do your unique readers have?
What products/services are your unique readers interested in?
Why do they read your book instead of other publications that are pursuing the same readers?
Does your magazine get read or skimmed?
How does your magazine break through the clutter?
How do you keep your readers loyal?
How well do you penetrate your market?

**Business to business publication**
Which SIC codes are you targeting?
How many businesses in each SIC code?
What's the size of the average business?
What are their annual sales?
How many employees do they have?

**Consumer publication**
What are the demographics of the principle and pass along readers?
What is the household income?
What is their education?
Describe the family unit?

Once you understand your readers, their unique interests and their buying power it's easy to identify clients that will benefit from advertising in your publication. In other words, instead of calling on anyone that might deal with your market you can increase your success by calling on those advertisers that have the most to gain.

**R**eader **I**ndustry **C**lient **C**ompetition

# I Industry expert

## You must become an expert in <u>your</u> industry

Today's busy decision makers don't want to waste their valuable time meeting with a magazine salesperson whose knowledge is limited to information published in the media kit. They want to work with someone they can rely on to gain insight and advice; someone that can provide industry details and stats they cannot readily get from any other source; someone that will help them reach their sales and marketing objectives. So it's vital that you fully understand your industry and that you keep up with your industry's ever changing trends.

Here's an example of what I mean. How would the average sales rep, working for *Leisure Travel Magazine* and calling on tour operators, fare when selling against Mr. Ricc, an industry expert who instead of just repeating the stats in the media kit could share the following information with his new prospect.

How are leisure travel decisions made?
What is the role of price?
Is budget always top of mind?

How much was spent on leisure travel last year?
What is this year's forecast?
What are the demographics of the leisure traveler?
What is their annual household income?
What are the current travel trends?
What are the new travel destinations?
Who regulates the travel industry?
What new regulations are in the works?
Who are the big leisure travel spenders?
What is their life style?
What is the average expenditure for the leisure traveler?
How are trips being booked? (Internet, travel agents, etc.)
What amenities is the leisure traveler looking for?
What percentage are renting cars?
What age group do guided tours appeal to?
What hotel amenities are they looking for?
How important is safety?

Not only would the prospect be impressed by Ricc's industry insight, but Ricc's extensive knowledge would create a paradigm shift. Instead of being viewed as a salesperson, Ricc would be perceived as a valuable resource. And if Ricc now showed the prospect that these industry stats, describe his publication's unique readers, selling advertising would suddenly become easy.

**Steps to success**
One of the fastest ways to gain insight into your industry is through your industry's association. So visit their website on regular bases, read the articles and stay on top of changes and trends.

**R**eader **I**ndustry **C**lient **C**ompetition

# C Client's industry

## You must become an expert in <u>your client's</u> industry

Clients don't want to deal with an advertising salesperson, they want to deal with an industry expert who understands *their* business and can help them reach their sales and marketing goals.

For example, if you were the marketing manager at a company that sold office supplies, who would you prefer to deal with; someone who represented a business publication or an individual that understands the office supply industry; an expert that is familiar with your challenges, your market and your competitors?

Everybody wants to work with the industry expert, so if you want to make selling easy take the time to learn about your client's products/services and customers. Here are just some of the questions you should be able to answer.

How is the client's product/service positioned in the industry?
How is the product/service sold? (retail, distributors, direct sales, website)

Is the product/service sold regionally or nationally?
What is the size of the client's market?
What is the client's market share?
Who buys the client's product/service?
Who influences the decision maker?
What marketing services is the client presently using? (direct mail, radio, trade shows, magazine ads)
How is the client using his website? (sell product, branding, lead generation)
How is the client driving traffic to his website or retail location?
Who are the client's major competitors?
Who is #1 in the client's industry?
What is the client's marketing position?
How are his competitors marketing their products?
What image is the client portraying in his marketing collateral?
Is the product/service seasonal? (when is high and low season?)
Is the client launching a new product?
What challenges is the client's industry facing?
What are the industry trends?
Does the client support a co-op marketing program?

**Steps to success**
So before calling on a new account;

- Contact your client's association to learn about the industry and trends.
- Call on the client's distributors or retailers to find out what sells and what challenges they are facing.
- Contact the client's salespeople to gather insider's information. They can tell you about

previous marketing results, upcoming campaigns and new product launches.

Learning about your client's industry will give you a huge competitive edge, but gaining this expertise takes time, so instead of randomly calling on every prospect that would benefit from advertising in your publication focus on one industry at a time. (See "Focus on one vertical market" page 115)

**R**eader **I**ndustry **C**lient **C**ompetition

# C Competition

## Know your competition

Your competitor is not just another magazine. It could be radio, television, billboards and trade shows but most often you'll find yourself competing against direct mail and the web.

**Competitive magazines**

You can't sell against a competitive magazine if you don't know what you are up against, so instead of just reading your competitor's media kit, study it. You need to identify their weaknesses but most important you need to know about their strengths.

Do they have stronger editorial content, a higher distribution or a lower CPM? What merchandising offers are they using to stimulate sales? Are they better established? Do they have a higher readership? Is their circulation audited? Which clients have they lost over the past 12 months? Which clients have they gained?

Now here's a word of caution. All publications have strengths and weaknesses so don't try to hide the fact that your publication may be weak in some areas. For example, if it is common knowledge that your competitor has stronger editorial content don't try to persuade the prospect that your editorials are just as strong, instead turn a weakness into strength by boasting about it.

*Mr. Prospect, you're absolutely right our competitors are known for their strong editorial content; whereas we're known as the publication that decision makers turn to when making a purchase. Isn't that what you are looking for?*

*Mr. Prospect, over 87% of our clients renew their campaign every year; not because of our editorial content but rather because our publication generates the best response. Isn't that what you are really looking for?*

Although you should take advantage of another publication's weakness, keep in mind that your prospects are more interested in hearing what your publication can do, than they are in listening to what your competition is lacking; so focus on benefits.

**Web marketing**

It's probably fair to say that every one of your prospects has a website and they've already discovered that a website is a great marketing tool that can be used to generate leads, sell product, build customer loyalty and disseminate information. So today's marketing managers and owners are not interested in listening to a presentation that tries to convince them that magazine advertising is better than web marketing. Instead they want to know how magazine ads can be used to help them reach their web marketing goals.

Make sure that your prospects understand that the biggest benefit to the web - it allows customers that are looking to buy their products/services instant access - is also the web's biggest drawback; the web offers choice. In other words, unless the customer is looking for a specific brand or company the customer is just as likely to order from a competitor's website as from your prospect.

So instead of positioning your publication as an alternative to web marketing, show your prospects that magazine advertising is the perfect vehicle for building brand identity and that will drive traffic to their website.

**Direct mail**

With few exceptions the only time that direct mail will win over magazine advertising is if the prospect is trying to reach a highly defined market, in which case advertising in your publication would result in paying for a large wasted circulation. So to effectively deal with a prospect that is weighing the benefits of direct mail against magazine advertising you must have a clear understanding of the relationship between your unique readers and the prospect's customers; you must become Mr. Ricc.

If there's a strong fit between your book and the prospect's customers then magazine advertising is easy to defend.

*Magazine ads are more cost effective*
Do a CPM analysis and show the prospect that direct mail is more expensive than magazine advertising, especially when you add in the pass along readers.

*Magazine ads build brand image and customer loyalty*
While most of your prospects will consider a direct mail campaign that generates 2% - 5% response a success, they neglect to consider the 95-98% that didn't respond. Show the prospect that a direct response style ad, placed in your publication will not only generate immediate response, the ad will increase long term sales by building brand image and customer loyalty.

*Magazine ads attract decision makers*
For a business to business direct mail campaign to be effective it must reach the decision maker, but business decisions are rarely made unilaterally. To maximize response, the mailer should be sent to the individual that uses the product/service, the person he or she reports to and if it's a big ticket item the CFO and the president. This exercise can double or even quadruple the prospect's direct mail cost and even then there's no guarantee that the mailer will reach the right person because titles are often misleading.

While direct mail struggles to get noticed by decision makers, an ad placed in a trade publication with the right editorial content will attract these hard to reach customers.

# Who should you call on, the agency or the client?

# The problem with advertising agencies

Here's the problem you face when dealing with an advertising agency. An advertising agency invests a considerable amount of time and effort evaluating and identifying different marketing options, to determine, what *they believe* to be, the best media to promote their client's products or services. They then meet with the client and make a detailed presentation that assures the client that they've done their due diligence by evaluating all the options before recommending which media should carry the client's ads.

Despite the fact that your publication may be ideally suited to promote their client's product/service;

- if the agency decided to use another media such as direct mail instead of magazine ads, or
- if you meet with the advertising agency after they have made a media presentation to the client,

it is highly unlikely that they will consider your book. After all, they would have to go back and tell the client their initial recommendations were incorrect – that they now have a better idea.

Also keep in mind that advertising agencies rarely select an individual magazine; they create a plan that could easily include 5 different books plus direct mail and an email campaign. So even though your magazine may reach their target market, when viewed as part of their overall marketing plan, your publication may not be that important.

Once a media plan has been created the easiest way and in most cases the only way to get your publication added to the plan is to deal directly with the client.

# Sell the client, tell the agency

Here's the bottom line, if you can't sell the client on the advantages of advertising in your publication, there's little chance you'll be successful with the ad agency. Although you may eventually end up dealing with the ad agency, to be successful in advertising sales you must always call on the client first.

If you can show the marketing manager, sales manager or president how your publication will help them increase sales and reach their marketing objectives they'll want to do business with you and that will force the advertising agency to look at your publication, even after they've finalized their media plan.

Your objective is to sell the client and tell the agency; but as a minimum to stimulate conversation about your publication between the client and the agency.

Only call on the agency if the client refuses to commit to your advertising strategy without the agency's involvement.

# Dealing with ad agencies

# Don't go client hunting

All too often salespeople take a backwards approach when calling on ad agencies. They contact the agency to tell them about their wonderful publication. They give a detailed and inspiring description of their reader demographics and attention getting articles. They outline their editorial calendar and then they end their presentation by saying *"Do you have any clients that would benefit from advertising in our publication?"*

Now they expect the ad agency to go through their client list, find a fit, call on the client and sell the publication. In other words, they're asking the agency to do the selling for them and in most cases that will not happen.

So don't go client hunting. Before calling on the agency find out which clients they represent and only call on the agency if there is a perfect fit between one of their clients and your publication.

# What agencies want to hear

**They don't want to know about your magazine**
Unless you can demonstrate a strong fit between your publication and the agency's client, don't even try to solicit an ad, and if there is a strong fit it's your job to prove it. So instead of telling the agency about your magazine, show them exactly how your book will help them move their client's business ahead.

**Don't repeat what's in your media kit**
When meeting with the agency don't waste their time telling them what they can read in your media kit.

**They want more market information**
Ad agencies work on numerous accounts at the same time which means they can only dedicate limited resources and time to familiarize themselves with each of their client's markets. So more often than not they'll welcome Mr. Ricc, an industry expert that can provide valuable solutions, ideas, statistics and insights that will give them a better understanding of their client's marketplace. Position yourself as the industry expert they're looking for by telling them something they can't hear from any other source.

**They want claims to be supported by stats**
Keep in mind that an ad agency is accountable so they can't afford to make flippant decision; they need very, very strong reasons for everything they

do. Your job is to give them those strong reasons, so whenever possible support your claims with statistics.

**They don't want to hear about other magazines**
Don't waste their time telling them what other magazines can't do, instead focus on telling them what you can do and how that will benefit their client.

**They don't want to buy an ad**
Although your book may reach their client's target market, as part of their overall marketing plan, placing an ad in your publication may not be all that important, so don't call on them to sell an ad. Instead help them put together a plan; a strategy that will allow them to meet their client's marketing goals. In other words, stop selling magazine ads and start offering multi-tiered solutions. (See "The Ad Shuffle" page 186)

# Call on the account executive first

The account executive's function is to maintain and grow the relationship between the client and the agency. Account executives not only work with their clients to define marketing and communication problems and to develop solutions, they also listen to their clients and are influenced by their client's interests. If the client shows a preference towards magazine advertizing – and better still towards your publication – there's a strong chance that your magazine will become part of the agency's media plan. So as I've already mentioned, always sell the client and tell the agency.

If the client insists that you deal with their advertising agency, find out who the account executive is and contact this individual first. While the account executive doesn't want to waste his time meeting with ad salespeople who are fishing for client information, as soon as he realizes you are already dealing with his client and that you've developed a strategy that will help the client reach their marketing objective he'll want to meet with you.

**Next call on the media supervisor**
Only after you've sold the client and the account executive should you approach the media department.

The media department does not establish a target market nor does this department decide if magazines, radio, television or direct mail will be used to drive the advertising campaign.

If magazines are part of the campaign then their job is to shortlist the selected publications by comparing reader demographics, circulation, editorial content and CPM. To ensure your book becomes part of the final media plan you need to influence this department.

Instead of just mailing a media kit, contact the media supervisor, tell him about your meeting with the client and the account executive and make a strong presentation that justifies your CPM and clearly shows him the benefits of adding your publication to the campaign.

# Sending media kits to agencies

Wouldn't it be nice if all you had to do was to send your information packed media kit to every ad agency and watch the insertion orders roll in? Unfortunately it doesn't work that way, so as a rule of thumb, you should only send a media kit if you cannot arrange a face to face meeting.

**Media kits don't sell**

Advertising agencies don't have the time to study the hundreds of media kits they receive each year so most of them never get read. And even if your media kit does grab their attention, do you really believe they're going to read the entire package and analyze the data in the hope they'll find a fit between your publication and one of their clients? At most, they'll give your media kit a cursory glance and if the pertinent information doesn't jump off the page the kit will be discarded.

**Your media kit must focus on one client**

Don't send a generic media kit and expect the ad agency to study it and find a fit with one of their clients. If you're sending a media kit to an ad agency, the information in the kit and accompanying cover letter must be tailored to address the marketing needs of one specific client. So only include the marketing data that is relevant to that client.

# Going over the agency's head

What should you do if your book is perfect for the client yet, the ad agency refuses to consider your publication? Is it acceptable to go over the agency's head and call directly on the client?

Advertising agencies don't like it. They don't want you meddling with their clients – especially after they've already told you they are not interested in your publication. Which means, although you could go over their head, doing so is not in your best interest.

Sell the client first and you'll rarely, if ever, find yourself in this situation, because if the client is sold on the benefits of advertising in your publication the agency will include it in their media plan.

If the agency shows no interest in your publication it either means that; your publication is not reaching their target audience or you have not sold the client.

# Selling co-op ads

Many manufacturers use co-op advertising to bring their national campaigns down to the local level. While the manufacturer may provide the funds and creative materials the onus is on the retailer or dealer to place the ads. But since most retailers and dealers are not marketing savvy, many don't take advantage of co-op marketing opportunities, and every year billions of co-op dollars go unspent.

Here's what you need to know to go after this lucrative sales opportunity.

**Co-op dollars are usually a percentage of purchases**

For example, a dealer or retailer that buys $200,000 worth of goods from the manufacturer may be entitled to 3% co-op dollars which equals $6,000 in advertising funds.

**Co-op dollars have a limited shelf life**

It is not uncommon for a manufacturer to stipulate that co-op funds can only be accumulated and must be spent within a calendar year, in which case co-op funds that are not spent by the end of December will be forfeited.

**Co-op advertising expenditures are usually shared**

While some manufacturers will allow the use of co-op dollars to pay for up to 100% of the media cost of the ad, a 50/50 split is more common, which means that a dealer or retailer who spends $8,000 on media can claim up to $4,000 under the co-op program.

# Presentations that sell

# Stop sending media kits

More often than not, sending a media kit will reduce your chances of landing the account.

Most media kits are extremely informative so anyone that receives one will believe they now have all the information they need to make an informed buying decision, so they don’t need to talk to you.

Furthermore, a media kit can’t make a strong presentation that shows the prospect all the benefits of advertising in your magazine; the kit can’t address your prospect’s questions and concerns and it can’t justify your CPM; only you can do this. So stop sending media kits.

With few exceptions, only mail a media kit after all attempts to get an appointment have failed.

# Don't include a rate card in your media kit

As I've just mentioned, stop sending media kits, but if you must send a media kit, then at least stay in control of the sale by *not* including a rate card.

Here's why you must leave out the rate card.

1. When a prospect receives a media kit he always looks at the rate card first and if he feels that the posted rate is too high, he'll immediately discount your magazine from further consideration. In other words, he will not study the media kit and look for benefits that could justify the price.

2. To be successful in ad sales you must meet with the prospect and make a presentation that shows the benefits of advertising in your publication. Including a rate card in your media kit makes it difficult to get an appointment. After all, the prospect now has all the information he needs to make a decision, so why should he waste time meeting with or even talking to a salesperson. When you send a media kit without a rate card the prospect must call you to get this information and that gives you an opportunity to sell.

# The media kit follow-up call

When you contact a prospect after sending a media kit never say *"Did you receive the media kit I mailed last week?"* or *"Have you had a chance to look at the media kit?"* because the prospect will often turn your question into an opportunity to brush you off by saying *"No"* or *"I haven't had a chance to look at it yet, so call me back in a few weeks"*. As you've probably noticed, when you call back in a few weeks you usually get the same response.

When making a follow-up call, don't ask the prospect about the media kit; instead, make a short presentation that piques his interest and setup an appointment.

# Never hand out a media kit at the beginning of a meeting

All too often we begin the meeting by handing the prospect a media kit and rate card and then continue by saying *"Let me tell you about our publication and marketing services."*

Although you may then follow through with a strong presentation, you no longer have the prospect's attention, because the moment you hand the prospect a media kit the prospect feels that he has all the information he needs to make an informed decision; so he no longer needs to listen to you.

The only time to hand out a media kit is at the end of the presentation and even then *do not* include a rate card.

# You can't make money selling ads

Although you might be able to convince a prospect to run an ad, even though your publication may not be the best vehicle to promote his product or service, doing so is a complete waste of time and effort because you can't make money selling one offs.

To make money in ad sales you need to have a book of clients that will continue to run ads and increase their space buys each year, because the ads are bringing measurable results.

So before calling on a new prospect make sure there is a strong fit between your publication and the prospect's products and services.

# How to build credibility and trust

We all know that the secret to building a strong house that will last for generations is to build it on a solid foundation because if the foundation can't support the weight of the structure the house will eventually crumble.

In advertising sales, credibility and trust is the foundation upon which the sale is built because the effectiveness of your presentation and your ability to influence the prospect is directly proportional to your credibility. If your credibility is not well established – if the prospect doesn't trust you – he will not invite you to his office and he will not place an ad.

Corralling, Status Matching and Echoing are proven and tested techniques that will help you build a strong sales foundation.

# Corralling

Your prospects are more interested in what their competitors are doing than they are in your unique and new ideas. In other words, they are more worried about being left behind than they are about leading the pack.

For example, if the prospect suspects that some of his competitors are successfully using your publication to drive customers to their website, generate leads or enhance branding he'll be concerned that your publication is giving them a competitive advantage. On the other hand, if none of his competitors are using your services he'd be more reluctant to run an ad. Likewise if he believes, even if only in the back of his mind, that his competitors are getting results from your merchandising offers, he'll want to know more about these marketing opportunities.

You can take advantage of your prospect's interest in knowing what his competition is doing and establish credibility with a technique called Corralling. Corralling simply means; giving the prospect the impression that many of his competitors are already successfully using your services so it's in his best interest to see what you have to offer. There are a number of different ways to create a Corralling effect.

1. Tell the prospect about other clients *in his industry* who are already on onboard. While

three or four names will suffice, the longer the list the better, in fact 6 or 7 names is ideal.

2. If you don't have any clients in his industry you can still create a Corralling effect by saying *We deal with companies like yours.*

3. As soon as you've landed an appointment with a new prospect in his industry you can create a Corralling effect by sharing this information with your next prospect. *Mr. Prospect, I was just talking to Fred over at ABC manufacturing, you may know him.*

**Steps to success**

Don't make random calls; instead focus on one vertical market at a time. Make a list of all existing clients within that vertical market and use this list to create a Corralling effect.

# Status Matching

A company president or owner is unlikely to sit down with the caretaker to discuss a business plan, likewise a marketing manager believes that his marketing problems are best understood by another marketing expert and a media buyer feels that other individuals in his field can best understand his challenges; because **people of authority prefer to deal with people of equal status**.

Herein is the reason that many salespeople are reluctant to call on upper management. Their gut feeling tells them that, president and salesperson is not a good match - and they are right. Executives don't want to deal with salespeople; they want to deal with industry experts that understand *their* unique business and marketing problems. To gain the credibility you need to deal with upper management you must reposition your status to match theirs.

Status is derived from title or association. Here are some examples.

- Having a PhD instills instant status, respect and credibility. The title alone makes everything this individual says more credible.
- A writer for The Harvard Business Review instantly gains the status of this prestigious publication by association and this makes everything this individual says more credible.

- Irrespective of his or her academic background, someone who sits on the board of the Law Society, instantly gains the status of this establishment by association, which makes everything this individual says more credible.

Although most of us don't have the title to stand head-to-head with the director of marketing or CFO, we can all gain equal status by experience and association.

1. **Experience**
   Tell the prospect how long you have been working in the industry and what you've accomplished for others. For example;

   *Ted, over the past 5 years I've worked with dozens of companies in your industry. In fact just last year I made some recommendations that helped Bob at ABC Enterprises generate over 200 new leads and increase sales by 6%.*

2. **Association**
   While experience is important, who gained from your experience is equally important. For example, telling the president about all the wonderful things you did for the media buyer at another company, tells him that you spend your time working with buyers. Although you might understand that individual's needs, you don't necessarily understand the needs and concerns of upper management; you don't have the status to deal with the president so you'd better go see the buyer. But you can instantly gain the status you need to be respected by your prospects, by

telling them about other people of equal status that you've dealt with.

**To president**
*Ted, I was just talking to Susan King, you might know her, she's the* <u>*president*</u> *of Excel Manufacturing.*

**To marketing manager**
*Fred, I was just talking to Bob Baxter, you might know him, he's the* <u>*marketing manager*</u> *over at Excel Manufacturing.*

**To sales manager**
*Susan, I was just talking to Bill Smith, you might know him, he's the* <u>*sales manager*</u> *over at Excel Manufacturing.*

**Steps to success**
Create a list of key contacts in each vertical market and use these contact names to status match.

# Building trust

Studies have shown that when meeting someone for the first time, our initial attitude towards the individual is primarily based on *likeness*. The more we have in common with someone the more likely we are to lower our guard. From a sales perspective this insight is of paramount importance because until the prospect trusts you, you're talking to deaf ears, so the sooner you build trust the sooner you'll make the sale.

**Likeness leads to trust**

Likeness goes far beyond clothing and external appearance. Most of us already know that we need to dress for the occasion so there's no need for me to elaborate on this point, but likeness also refers to behavioral preferences. When we exhibit the same traits as our prospects, they get the feeling that we are alike and that we look at their problems in the same way they do, and that opens the door to candid discussions where prospects willingly answer our probing questions and disclose their wants and concerns.

**Echo your prospect's verbal communication**

Dr. Albert Mehrabian, a leading researcher in body language, found that 38 percent of the power of what we say is not in the words themselves, but in how we say them. Which means that an informative presentation that offers your prospect a solution to his or her marketing problem is not necessarily enough to land the account; it's how you communicate your message that makes all the difference. Echoing is an advanced selling technique that allows you to gain your prospect's immediate trust by reflecting his or her behavioral preferences.

**Speed up or slow down**

We've all talked to a prospect whose speech pattern was exceptionally slow or fast and the longer we found ourselves in their presence the more uncomfortable we felt. As we listened to the slow talker we desperately wanted to jump in and finish the sentences.

Although we all speak at a different rate, each and every one of us believes that our rate of speech is the norm therefore we're quick to believe that people who speak at a different rate are different from ourselves. For example, the term "fast talker" is often used to describe someone who is untrustworthy while someone who speaks very slowly is often labeled as unintelligent.

Don't forget - likeness builds trust - so create likeness by pacing your speech pattern to your prospects. If your prospect speaks slowly or quickly, echo his speech pattern by matching his pace. This adjustment will make your prospects feel more comfortable with the dialogue and this is an important step in gaining their trust.

**Adjust the volume**

Although vocal modulation can and should be used to grab your prospect's attention and to show enthusiasm, for the most part the volume of your dialogue should echo your prospect. For example, a soft spoken individual is likely to feel un-comfortable and even intimidated in the company of a loud, boisterous salesperson so unless the salesperson adjusts the volume of his dialogue this difference can result in resistance, making selling difficult.

Echoing your prospect's vocal volume displays likeness and that builds trust because, as we already know, people prefer to deal with people that are like themselves.

# What benefits should you offer?

While credibility and trust is the foundation of the sale, benefits are the motivating force that will convince your prospects that it's time to switch marketing campaigns and give you their business. But the question remains *"What benefits should you offer?"*

The obvious answer is to ask probing questions that identify the prospect's needs, wants and concerns and then tailor your presentation accordingly. Unfortunately this solution encounters a major barrier.

- In order to identify the prospect's marketing problem and offer a benefit you need to meet with the prospect and ask probing questions.
- The prospect won't waste his time meeting with you and answering your probing questions unless you offer him a benefit first.
- You can't offer a benefit until you've asked probing questions that identify his marketing objectives.

Universal Wants are the key to overcoming this impasse.

Although all your prospects have individual needs and wants that can only be identified by asking probing questions, their individual wants are overshadowed by Universal Wants. Universal Wants stem from the prospect's need to fulfill the demands of his or her job.

Everyone you talk to has a job description and their status in the company is a direct reflection of their ability to meet or surpass their work obligations. For example, a marketing manager's performances will be measured by his or her ability to design successful marketing programs; a sales manager's performance will be measured by his ability to increase sales and a production manager's performance will be measured in output. Since most of your prospects are interested in meeting or surpassing their job obligations, identifying their Universal Wants is the key to piquing their interest.

# Understanding Ted, Aim, and Pam

Although you may deal with hundreds of different prospects they can all be grouped into three decision making categories; Ted, Aim, and Pam.

**TED** is an acronym for *Top Executive Decision Maker.*
Although Ted is usually the president or owner of the company, Ted could also be the head of a division. When dealing with Ted, keep in mind that he or she is not interested in advertising. In other words, Ted couldn't care less about circulation, editorial content, bonus marketing programs or CPM. Likewise, Ted is not interested in the fact that placing an ad in your publication will enhance branding and generate leads for his salespeople; Ted has managers that deal with these day-to-day business decisions. To uncover Ted's Universal Want ask yourself the following question.

*How does Ted measure his or her success?*

Ted's success is tied directly to the company's performance; therefore his or her primary interest is the bottom line. So if you expect Ted to grant you an appointment or approve your advertising schedule you'll need to show Ted how your suggestions and ideas will improve his or her financial position.

Here's a summary of Ted's characteristics.

- There is only one Ted per company
- Controls the budget
- Has veto power
- Is interested in benefits not features

Ted's Universal Want is to improve the bottom line.

**AIM** is an acronym for *Ad Impacts Me*
Aim represents all those individuals that personally stand to gain or lose by placing an ad in your publication. For example, Aim could be the marketing manager or the sales manager, because in many cases an ad campaign will affect them both. If the campaign generates a large number of leads and inquiries, both marketing and sales would shine. On the other hand, if the campaign generated little response, both individuals could be held accountable for their poor performance. So keep in mind that although the marketing manager may be sold on the advantages of advertising in your publication, if the sales manager doesn't like the idea, you'll have trouble closing the deal.

Like Ted, Aim is not interested in your magazine and contrary to popular belief he's not concerned with CPM. For example, Aim the marketing manager has placed a lead generating ad in a competitor's publication and he's getting 30 leads per month. Now remember that Aim's performance is not measured by how good the ad looks nor is he rewarded for reducing the CPM. Aim gains recognition by putting together an ad campaign that gets results and the better the response the higher the praise, therefore a suggestion to switch publications may be exactly what Aim is looking for.

Even though his CPM may increase, this is a trade-off that Aim will gladly accept if it results in a higher response and more sales. So instead of telling Aim about your publication, offer him solutions that will help him achieve his business goals and you'll get his attention.

Here's a summary of Aim's characteristics.

- There will likely be several Aim's per company
- Works within a defined budget
- Interested in benefits not features

Here are some examples of Universal Wants that will pique Aim's interest. To identify his actual wants you'll need to ask probing questions.

**Universal Wants**

| Marketing manager | Sales manager |
| --- | --- |
| Response | Sales |
| Leads | Leads |
| Sales | |
| Branding | |
| Market share | |

**PAM** is an acronym for *Purchasing Agent/Media Buyer*
Although Pam is usually a purchasing agent or media buyer, he or she could be any number of people such as an office administrator.

In most cases Pam has received detailed instructions from Aim or Ted and her job is to place the ad where they tell her to. So even though your publication may be better suited then her present choice, selling Pam is a waste of time because she doesn't have the authority to switch publications, consider new merchandising opportunities or make changes to the campaign without Ted's or Aim's approval.

Here's a summary of Pam's characteristics.

- Cannot make changes
- Receives direction from Ted or Aim
- Is interested in features not benefits

Pam's Universal Want is security, so Pam is always reluctant to try something new. When prospecting for new business never call on Pam.

**Steps to success**
Before contacting Ted and Aim identify their Universal Wants and use it to pique their interest.

# Identify all buying influences

A marketing manager rarely makes a unilateral decision; he'll most likely discuss your marketing proposal with the sales manager and president or get his advertising agency involved, and each of these buying influences has different interests. For example, the president is most likely interested in improving the bottom line, the sales manager in sales and the marketing manager in gaining market share and generating leads. Therefore you must identify all buying influences and make a presentation that shows each of them how your publication will help them reach their individual goals.

Here's a simple way to find out if there is more than one decision maker. At the end of your first meeting say,

*Mr. Prospect, if you don't mind me asking is there anyone else besides yourself involved in this decision making process? The reason I ask is if there is, I'd be happy to leave some extra media kits. How many kits would you like?*

If the prospect asks for more than one media kit then he's not the sole decision maker. Find out who the other media kits are for and be sure to put these individuals on your prospecting list.

# Establishing a budget

When dealing with existing clients, establishing a budget is not that important, however when calling on new prospects you must find out how much they can afford to spend before proposing a campaign.

Although you could simply say *"If you don't mind me asking, what's your marketing budget for this year?"* a more professional way to find this answer is to explore their previous spending habits, because in most cases this year's budget will be similar to last year's expenditure.

If magazine ads are already part of the prospect's marketing mix, establishing a budget is easy.

*Which publications did you advertise in last year?*
*How many issues did you advertise in last year?*
*What size ad did you usually run?*

If magazine ads are a new venture then you can establish a budget by exploring their previous marketing methods.

*What marketing collateral are you presently using? (Brochures, catalogues, newsletters, direct mail, etc.)*
*How often do send out the brochures?*
*How many do you mail each time?*

# Focus on the prospect's wants - not his needs

When you're meeting with a prospect who is interested in placing an ad, and your dialog focuses on questions like;

*What size ad are you considering?*
*How many colors?*
*Do you have a positioning preference?*
*In how many issues will the ad run?*
*When is the start date?*

you are selling to a prospect's *needs,* and when you sell to *needs* you are always selling price. In other words, your presentation is forcing the prospect to focus on CPM.

But as you already know, Ted and Aim are not interested in CPM; they're looking for someone who can help them reach their Universal Wants. So instead of asking questions about the ad, build credibility and pique the prospect's interest by focusing on the prospect's customers, marketing activities and business goals. Here are just a few sample questions.

*Is your primary objective to sell product or generate leads?*
*To what extent is branding important?*
*Which target markets are you focusing on?*
*What is their SIC code?*
*What size of businesses are you trying to reach?*
*Which features and benefits are most appealing to this target market?*

*What sales potential do you see in this market?*
*Do you sell your products direct or through dealers?*
*What support do you offer your dealers?*
*How are you presently reaching this market?*
- *Direct mail*
- *Catalogues*
- *Web marketing*
- *Trade shows*
- *Magazine ads (Which publications?)*
- *Salespeople*

*How do you generate leads for your salespeople?*
*Which decision maker(s) are you trying to reach?*
*Who do these decision makers report to?*
*Which product(s) will this campaign focus on?*
*Who are your major competitors?*
*Who is the market leader?*
*How are your competitors promoting their products?*
*What is your competitor's biggest strength?*
*What is your market share?*
*How do you drive traffic to your website?*
*What are the demographics of your target market?*
*What's their family income?*
*How will the reader respond to your ad?*
*How will you measure response?*
*What volume of response are you hoping to get?*

By the time you finish asking these questions you should be able to say,

*So you <u>want</u> to influence chartered accountants at manufacturing plants with 150 or more employees.*

or

*So you want to appeal to female home owners, 35 to 55 years old with a household income of $100,000 or more who are planning to remodel their kitchen.*

Once you have a clear understanding of exactly what your prospect *wants* you can make a strong presentation that shows him how advertising in your publication will allow him to reach his business and marketing goals.

**Steps to success**

So select a target market and using the above as a guideline write 30 questions that will identify the prospect's wants.

# Prospect will not translate features into benefits

Features tell your prospects about your publication, readers and merchandising services. Benefits show them how your publication, readers and merchandising services will allow them to reach their business and marketing goals.

When making a presentation, always keep in mind that your prospects will not translate features into benefits. If you expect them to realize all the advantages your publication has to offer you must make this translation for them.

During your next presentation imagine that your prospect is wearing a large pointed hat and on the front of this hat, in bright red letters, are the words **"So what?"** Now, each time you mention a feature these words begin to flash.

*Mr. Prospect, our magazine has been delivering innovative ideas to independent retailers for over 12 years*. (feature) **So what?** *This means that our publication has the highest circulation*. (feature) **So what?** *This adds up to more sales and leads.* (benefit)

*Our publication provides comprehensive editorial coverage that is valued by top decision makers.* (feature) **So what?** *This means that we have the highest readership.* (feature) **So what?** *And that results in higher response.* (benefit)

*Our magazine is distributed only to a select target market and every non-paid subscriber must verify that they are part of this select target market.* (feature) **So what?** *This means that we reach the decision makers that order your product.* (feature) **So what?** *And that will result in increased sales.* (benefit)

*Our publication is distributed to over 20,000 decision makers each month.* (feature) **So what?** *Therefore our magazine has the highest market penetration.* (feature) **So what?** *This means that more decision makers will read your ad.* (feature) **So what?** *And that will result in higher sales and more profits.* (benefit)

*Your ad also includes a free listing in our product directory.* (feature) **So what?** *This promotes your product year round.* (feature) **So what?** *And that adds up to more sales*. (benefit)

**Steps to success**

To develop a powerful presentation, on a sheet of paper list 10 company/publication features and then write out the corresponding customer benefit.

# Selling is not telling, selling is asking

We've all heard stories about those gifted sales-people who can sell anything to anyone. How do they do it?

Do these salespeople have special talents that allow them to sell against incredible odds or are they using high-pressure techniques to intimidate their prospects into buying? Neither. The reason these salespeople are so successful is because they recognize that the secret to closing is to give their prospects what they want.

What do your prospects want? Do they want to improve branding, generate leads for their salespeople, drive customers to their store or website, introduce a new product, increase sales or support their dealers? The list is endless and you have no way of knowing unless you ask, so before making a presentation always ask the prospect a series of probing questions that identify his or her wants and concerns. In fact, during a one hour meeting, 50 minutes should be spent asking questions and listening, because selling is not telling, selling is asking.

# Diagnose before you prescribe

It is fair to say that the diagnostic stage is the most important part of your presentation; because it is during this stage that you gain your prospects' trust and confidence by showing them that you are an industry expert who truly understands their unique marketing needs. So even though you may recognize, within the first two minutes, that your publication is perfectly positioned to help the prospect gain market share, generate leads and increase sales, you must resist the temptation to instantly make a recommendation.

Keep in mind, that landing a new account does not so much depend upon your ability to analyze the prospect's needs and make the right recommendation, as it does on your prospect believing that your recommendation is the right one.

Here's what I mean. Imagine you're driving to work when suddenly the engine starts to sputter. As the situation gets worse you pull into the service center of a large dealership. After briefly explaining your problem to the service manager he hands you a work order and says *"Another customer just had the same problem with his car. All we need to do is replace your fuel pump and your car will run fine. If you would just sign here, we'll get started on your car right away."*
*"But don't you think you should run some tests before making this repair?"* you ask.

*"No need to"* he replies *"As I mentioned, a new fuel pump solved their problem so I'm sure it will also solve yours."*

Would you sign the work order? Probably not, but why would you hesitate? The service manager is an experienced professional who knows what he's doing, so replacing the fuel pump may well solve your problem.

The reason you'd be reluctant to okay this repair is because the service manager failed to gain your confidence. It's difficult to believe someone's recommendations are well-founded when they don't take the time to diagnose the problem before prescribing a solution. So always ask probing questions before making a recommendation.

# Your prospects don't want choices

Imagine for a moment that you are visiting your doctor because of a stomachache. After a brief examination the doctor says *"I have several different medications that you could try. You have a choice between an antibiotic, an antacid or a muscle relaxant. I also need to know what strength you would prefer."*

Chances are that you would instantly lose respect for this doctor, because you expect him to make these decisions for you. After all, he is the professional.

As an advertizing/marketing professional and industry expert you should also be making decisions for your prospects. Instead of asking your prospect if she prefers a half or a full page ad; whether she wants to run in 3 or 6 issues or on which page she would like to place her ad, you must make these decisions for her. There is only one *best way* to promote the prospect's product/service and it is your responsibility to recommend the best, because your prospects don't want marketing choices, they want to deal with an industry expert who can provide solutions.

# Show your prospects that you know more about advertising than they do

If your idea of a presentation is to show the prospect a sample of your magazine, review the contents in the media kit and outline your editorial calendar, you're going to find selling a difficult challenge. This type of presentation does not encourage the prospect to engage. The prospect is not going to bring you into his world and candidly discuss his business and marketing objectives because he quickly realizes that you have little or nothing new to offer.

But the moment your prospects begin to see that you know something they don't, you become invaluable and they'll begin to share their concerns and listen to your recommendations and that makes selling easy.

So one of the primary objectives of your presentation is to show your prospects that you know more about advertising then they do.

# Ask probing questions before beginning your presentation

Unless you ask probing questions you have no way of knowing what your prospects want; furthermore the probing stage of the presentation is where you build credibility and trust and establish yourself as an industry expert. So always ask probing questions before commencing your presentation, even if you are already familiar with the prospect's business and marketing objectives.

To show the prospect that you already have an understanding of his business, rephrase your questions so that you're looking for affirmation instead of searching for an answer.

*Mr. Prospect, correct me if I'm wrong, but my understanding is that you are selling your products wholesale and that you have 43 dealers in North America.*

*I also understand that your sales peak in June and July and that you are trying to grow sales on your website. Is that correct?*

# Show your prospects that answering your questions is in their best interest

If you expect your prospects to participate in your probing exercise you must show them that answering your probing questions is in their best interest. In other words, offer them a benefit.

*Ms Prospect, at Best Publishing we've been helping companies like yours, increase sales and gain market share for over 15 years. If I can just ask you a few brief questions, I could share some ideas that other companies are already using to get these results.*

Who benefits from answering your questions? The prospect does and when there is something in it for them, they'll tell you anything you want to know.

# Your probing questions must be pre-planned

Could you sit down with the marketing manager at a new account and on the spot, ask 30 pertinent probing questions that identify his marketing and business objectives? Unfortunately most of us could not, so to maximize the benefit of this questioning period, you must pre-plan your probing questions – you must write them out before meeting with the prospect.

**Steps to success**
Create a set of probing questions for each vertical market you are calling on. Also prepare questions for different decision makers. For example, the probing questions you would ask a marketing manager would be slightly different from the questions you would ask the president or sales manager.

# Pique the prospect's interest

Here's where top income earners really differentiate themselves. While most salespeople try to impress their prospects by sharing ideas and offering solutions, top income earners know that sharing ideas is the fastest way to lose control of the sale. The prospect now has the information he needs to make a decision, so he no longer needs to listen to you.

Curiosity, not solutions, is what holds your prospects' attention and keeps them interested in your presentation. So top income earners never share ideas until the prospect is ready to buy; instead their presentation is designed to build curiosity by piquing the prospect's interests.

Here are 3 ways to pique your prospect's interest.

1. Show your expertise by asking expert questions.
2. Provide new information.
3. Cast doubt on the prospect's decisions.

# Ask expert questions

Don't forget, your prospects want to deal with Mr. Ricc, an industry expert, and the most effective way to show your expertise is to ask expert questions. So use your probing questions to show the prospect that you have an in-depth understanding of his or her industry.

Instead of asking technical questions which relate to the ad, ask diagnostic questions that focus on the prospect's marketing and business objectives.

# Provide new information

Your prospects don't want to hear old news. Old information is something they believe they should already know, so to avoid appearing uninformed, they'll act as if they've already considered this information. Here's an example of what I mean.

Salesperson: *Mr. Prospect, at Best Publishing we've been helping marketing managers gain market share for over 15 years.*

Prospect: *I'm not interested. I'm familiar with your publication.*

The Power of New: *Mr. Prospect, I understand but from time to time we develop some* ***new*** *marketing concepts that could increase sales and help you gain market share. All I'm suggesting is that you evaluate these* ***new*** *ideas.*

Notice how the word *new* piques the prospect's interest and encourages the prospect to reconsider his position.

# Cast doubt

Casting doubt is an extremely effective technique that will pique interest and open dialogue by showing your prospects that you know more about advertising than they do. Here are some examples.

**Cast doubt on positioning**
*Mr. Prospect, do you mind if I ask why you've requested that your ad be placed on the right side? The reason I ask is that many of my clients used to have the same request but they switched to a much more effective way to increase readership and response. Would you mind if I shared some ideas?*

**Cast doubt on specs**
*Mr. Prospect, I'd be happy to quote this ad exactly the way it is, but based on my experience working with other manufacturers, I'd like to make some recommendations that could increase readership and maximize response. Would that be okay?*

**Cast doubt on CPM**
*Mr. Prospect, although cost per thousand is an important consideration, many of my clients changed their focus to a more accurate indicator of an ad's success. Would you mind if I shared some recommendations?*

**Cast doubt on circulation**
*Mr. Prospect, although magazine circulation is important, there is a much more important factor to consider. Would you mind if I shared this ideas.*

## Cast doubt on other marketing methods

*Mr. Prospect, many of my clients used to use direct mail but they have switched to a much more cost effective way to generate leads for their salespeople. Would you mind if I shared some of these ideas?*

*Ms. Prospect, I've helped a number of my clients reduce their marketing cost while increasing their sales and leads. Would you mind if I shared some ideas?*

*Ms. Prospect, a number of my clients used to run ads in that same publication, but have since found a more effective way to market their products. Would you mind if I shared some ideas?*

*Mrs. Prospect, many of my clients used to use email campaigns to drive customers to their website but are now using a more effective method. Would you mind if I shared some ideas?*

# Never mention the price until you are ready to close

In today's marketplace, would you consider $50,000 a reasonable price for a house? Would you consider $10,000 to be a fair price for a car? You can't answer these questions until you know exactly what you are getting. Is the house located in a major city? Is it 900 square feet or 5,000? Is the car a 20 year old Lada or a brand new Cadillac?

This same logic holds true when selling magazine ads. Unless your prospects know exactly what they are getting for their investment, they can't judge the value. This means, if someone phones and says *"I'm interested in placing an ad in your publication. What's the cost for a ¼ page, 2 color ad that runs in 4 issues?"* don't quote a price.

Instead, ask probing questions that identify the prospect's marketing objectives and then make a complete presentation before giving a price. Here's a transition statement that will open dialogue and allow you to ask probing questions.

*Mr. Prospect, I'd be happy to give you a price but to ensure that you are getting the best price let me ask you a few brief questions.*

Notice that this transition statement offers the prospect a benefit for answering your questions, and if there's something in it for them they'll tell you anything you want to know.

# Bring your readers to life

Bringing your readers to life is the key to ad sales success, so instead of just rhyming off stats, use demographics, editorial content and circulation to create a picture that your prospect can relate to; a picture that shows there is a strong connection between your readers and the prospect's customers.

# Presenting editorial content

Although we would like to think that ad agencies and prospects are impressed by our publication's strong editorial content, they are not interested. So telling them about your first class writers and showing them your editorial calendar is a complete waste of time unless you follow through with the all important step and clearly show them that there is a direct connection between your editorial content and their marketing objectives. To make this connection you must be able to answer the following 4 questions.

1. How does your unique editorial content attract readers who are interested in their products?
2. How does your unique editorial content attract readers who can purchase their products?
3. How does your unique editorial content attract readers who can influence buying decisions?
4. How will your strong editorial content increase readership of their ad?

# Presenting demographics

Contrary to popular belief, ad agencies and prospects are not interested in your reader's demographics. In fact telling them about your reader's age, title, education, lifestyle and income is a complete waste of time unless these demographics describe your prospect's customers.

In other words, don't rhyme off these statistics and expect the agency or prospect to translate them into benefits that will help them reach their marketing goals. It's your job to clearly show them how advertising in your publication will help them increase sales, generate leads, drive customers to their website, gain market share and improve branding, which means that you need to have a clear picture of who your prospect's customers are before talking about your reader's demographics.

Also keep in mind that a prospect who is offering several different products may have customers with slightly different demographics. (See "Your clients want to deal with Mr. Ricc" page 11)

# Presenting circulation

Your prospects are not interested in the fact that your magazine is read by over 20,000 every month; they want to know how many of those 20,000 are interested in buying their products or services and that these reads can afford to make a purchase. So before talking about circulation you need to know who your prospect's customers are, because only then can you explain your publication's role in the buying process – as related to their product.

Remember your prospects are more interested in the number of potential customers than they are in your circulation.

# Paid vs. controlled circulation

The assumption is that if someone is willing to make a financial commitment and pay for a subscription, the magazine's readership would be higher. This means that when all things are equal, most advertisers would give preference to the magazine with the higher paid subscription – but rarely, if ever, are all things equal.

Most trade publications only have about 10% paid circulation, so more important than the number of readers that paid for the publication is the quality of the magazine's readers. That's why advertisers usually prefer to deal with a controlled circulation. After all, anyone can buy a subscription, but only those who meet the magazine's strict criteria will be part of a controlled circulation – and the key words are *strict criteria.*

When selecting a magazine, advertisers will generally put their money in the publication that has the tightest control over its circulation, so be prepared to prove that you have minimal wasted circulation. Here are some of the questions you must be able to answer.

What criteria do you use to qualify your subscriber?
Did the subscriber request the publication in writing?
How often do you update your circulation list?
How often are your readers required to renew their subscription?

# How to justify frequency

You can always go back to marketing 101 and explain that advertising is a process, not an event. Therefore, onetime ads rarely bring results and that studies have shown that the reader usually needs to see an ad five to six times before responding.

But a more effective way to sell frequency is to build it around the prospect's products/services and to do this you need to know the answer to the follow questions.

*Is the purpose of the ad to generate leads, sell product, drive retail or web activity, support dealers or branding?*
*How important is branding?*
*Does the prospect attend trade shows?*
*What is the product's/service's sales pattern?*
*Is the product used all-year round?*
*When are the peak periods?*
*Is the prospect launching a new product?*
*Is the prospect experiencing a sales slump?*
*How are the prospect's competitors marketing their product?*
*What is the frequency of the competitor's ads?*
*What is the prospect's budget?*

When dealing with prospects that have a limited budget, you can show your expertise by telling them they would do better if they run 6 ads over 6 months, than running 6 ads in 6 weeks.

# Don't tell the prospect about your merchandising services

How would you like to spend an hour with a prospect that walks you through his manufacturing plant and shows you all the wonderful upgrades that he's made over that past five years? You would probably lose interest very quickly.

Well, you can be sure that your prospects feel exactly the same way when you start telling them about your extensive marketing and merchandising services. The only services your prospects want to hear about are those that will help them reach their business and marketing goals.

So once again, make sure that you have an in-depth understanding of your prospect's products, customers and business objectives before presenting your marketing and merchandising services.

# Dealing with skepticism

No matter how well you disguise it, the fact remains that your job is to sell advertising and your prospect know it. So any claims – even though they may be 100% true – that your publication is the best; that you have the highest readership; the best editorials and that everyone who advertises with you is getting great results, will be met with skepticism and doubt. So you must be prepared to overcome this skepticism.

# Renewals overcome skepticism

Most of your prospects believe that their competitors would not be wasting money on ads that did not bring a measurable return, so one of the most effective ways to convince a prospect that adverting in your publication will generate great results is to tell the prospect about your renewal rate.

*At first every one of my clients was hesitant to place an ad – after all the question is does the return warrant the investment. Well, the answer lies in our renewal rate – over 87% of our clients renew their ad because promoting their products and services in our publication brings great results.*

*Over 91% of our advertisers renew their ad, not because we are the cheapest but rather because our publication generates the best return on investment. Isn't that what you are looking for?*

# Success overcomes skepticism

Testimonials turn claims into facts, so another effective way to persuade a skeptical prospect that adverting in your publication brings results is to tell him about the successes that other advertisers have achieved.

*I was just talking to Bob Baxter, you might know him; he's the marketing manager over at ABC Supplies. Last year we helped him increase his sales by over 15%.*

*We just completed a short audit and found that Jack over at ABC Wholesale generated 300 reader card inquiries from his 1/2 page ad.*

**Steps to success**
Compile an inventory of success stories and share these stories with your new prospects. Whenever possible, tell them about successes in *their* industry.

# Focus on ROI instead of CPM

While return on investment is the only reason that someone will advertise in your publication, ROI means different things to different prospects. For example, the president wants his ROI to have a positive effect on his bottom line, while the marketing manager may be looking for an increase in leads, sales or market share. So when making a presentation be sure to tailor the ROI to your prospect's interests.

*Wouldn't you agree that the effectiveness of your advertising campaign will be measured in response and sales not cost per thousand?*

*Over 90% of our clients renew their ads each year, not because we have the lowest CPM, but rather because our publication brings the highest return on investment. Isn't that what you are looking for?*

*Our clients are willing to accept a higher CPM because they know that our publication brings the highest ROI.*

*I know how you feel and many of my clients felt the same way. Initially they also focused on CPM. But after measuring response they found that our publication offered the best return on investment. Isn't that what you're really looking for?*

*We could reduce the CPM by cutting back on our editorial content but that would reduce readership and decrease your ROI.*

*We could lower the CPM by adding more small advertisers but that would result in clutter; take away from the visibility of your ad and decrease your ROI.*

# ROI is proportional to quality not quantity

Which of the following is the most effective; ad "A" which generated 100 leads or ad "B" which generated 20 leads? At first glance ad "A" is the clear winner, but now let's take sales into account. Ad "A" resulted in 5 sales, ad "B" resulted in 9 sales; now which ad is most effective?

Although leads and response are an important consideration, a more accurate measure of an ad's effectiveness is sales. Sales are directly proportional to the quality, not the quantity of the leads. So when a prospect claims he can generate a higher response from direct mail or a competitor's publication, draw this fact to his attention.

*Which is more important, the number of leads you generate or the resulting sales?*

*Our clients rely on our publication to generate the highest quality leads not the highest quantity. Isn't that what you are looking for?*

*Will the effectiveness of this ad campaign be measured by the quantity of leads generated or by the resulting sales?*

*Which would you rather have 200 poor leads or 100 highly qualified leads?*

# Increasing the size of your readership

Readership is comprised of two separate factors; *quality* and *quantity* and together or separately these factors can be used to justify why yours is the best publication.

*Quantity* refers to the number of *people* that actually read your magazine. For example, if your circulation is 15M but studies show your magazine is passed on to 2 additional readers, your readership is 45M.

When making a presentation focus on the total readership – which includes circulation plus, pass along readers - and use this total readership to calculate a lower CPM. For example, a $79 CPM, based on circulation would only be $25.33 CPM when pass along readership is factored in.

*Quality* refers to the number of potential *customers* who read your magazine and this number will vary from advertiser to advertiser. For example, your magazine and your competitor's publication are mailed to the same business to business, target market. But your competitor is winning clients by promoting the fact that they have higher market penetration - they have a 20M circulation and you only have 12M.

Although the competition clearly won the *quantity* battle, they could lose the war on the *quality* issue.

Find out who reads their magazine?
Do they have strong editorial content?
Who are their editorials directed at?
Is their magazine read or skimmed?

The answers to these questions could reveal that although you have a lower circulation, you have a *higher targeted readership.* In other words, more of your prospect's potential customers read your publication then read your competitors, which means that advertising in your publication will bring a higher return on investment.

# Focus on readership instead of circulation

One of the most effective ways to deal with prospects that are focused on circulation is to redirect their attention to readership.

Make sure that your prospects understand that circulation is only valuable when accompanied by targeted readership and that editorial content drives readership.

*Even the most powerful offer, directed at the right target market will generate no response until someone reads your ad, so readership is the key to success, and readership is directly proportional to editorial content.*

*Although circulation is important, the success of your campaign will depend on readership and the key to high readership is outstanding editorial content.*

*One of the most important considerations when selecting a magazine to run your campaign is editorial content, because outstanding editorials increase readership and the higher the readership the better the response.*

*Publishing a magazine is easy; motivating the recipient to read the publication is the real challenge and this can only be accomplished with high impact editorial content.*

*It's readership not circulation that generates sales and leads, and our publication has the highest readership in the industry. Isn't that what you are really looking for?*

*Our publication has fostered loyal readership by providing outstanding editorial content which ensures that your ad gets the highest exposure.*

*A targeted circulation will only bring great results when accompanied by high readership.*

*More important than the number of people who read your ad is the number of potential customers who read your ad and our publication has the highest targeted readership.*

# Boast about lower circulation

Don't try to hide the fact that your competitor's magazine has a higher circulation. Instead, turn your lower circulation into a benefit by boasting about it.

*We have access to the same mailing lists as our competitors so matching circulation would be easy. But we've specifically decided to clean our list and remove non-decision makers.*

*Over 90% of our clients renew their ads each year, not because we have the highest circulation, but rather because our publication brings the highest return on investment. Isn't that what you are looking for?*

*We could easily increase our circulation by sending our publication to non-decision makers and some publishers will take this road to reduce their CPM, but we believe in giving our clients a more accurate picture.*

*You could increase your circulation 10 fold by placing your ad in a newspaper instead of a trade publication, but as you know circulation is not the key to marketing success. The success of your campaign depends on 2 factors;*

- *reaching decision makers and*
- *readership*

*and it's here that our publication excels.*
*A higher circulation is only valuable if this extra circulation reaches additional decision makers. Wouldn't you agree?*

*Although our publication appears to have a slightly smaller circulation, we in fact reach more decision makers.*

*Our distribution only appears smaller because we have eliminated wasted circulation.*

*Even the highest circulation is of no value unless it is accompanied by readership and our publication has the highest readership in the industry.*

# Always create a sense of urgency

Consider the following scenario.

Prospect: *If I decided to go-ahead with this campaign, when would you need the artwork?*

Salesperson: *The publication closes in 3 weeks, so I need to have it by then.*

Although you may have sold the prospect on the benefits of placing an ad in your publication, a lot can happen during the next three weeks. The prospect could change his mind or he might shop around and get closed by the competition. Remember, if you don't give your prospects a reason to order today they won't, and time quickly kills desire; so always create a sense of urgency.

People want what they cannot get, so when the prospect shows interest in placing an ad or inquires about positioning, you have an excellent opportunity to close the sale by making these difficult to get.

**Make positioning difficult to get**
*I'm not sure that space is still available but let me check. If it is I'll immediately reserve it before someone else takes it.*

*I think the space opposite this article has already been sold but let me double check. If it's still available I'll reserve it immediately.*

**Make ad space difficult to get**

*We have 5 marketing consultants selling ad space for the spring issue so space sells quickly. To guarantee your place in that issue I'll have to reserve it immediately.*

*Because of the free upgrade promotion this is one of our most popular issues and it sells out quickly, so I'll reserve your ad space immediately.*

**Make price difficult to get**

*To take advantage of our 25% May discount I'll need to book your schedule immediately.*

**Make ad size difficult to get**

*This issue is just about sold out so I'm not sure that I can still book a ½ page ad, but let me check. If I can I'll reserve the space immediately.*

*I'd love to run your ½ page ad but I'm not sure that we still have that much space left but let me check. If it's available I'll reserve the space immediately.*

**Steps to success**

Make a list of 10 ways to create a sense of urgency and don't forget to consider any promotions that your publication may offer. For example;, buy 1 get 1 free, upgrades, special issues, discount pricing, bonus mailings, etc.

# Grow your client base

# 80% of all prospects will consider placing an ad

Fifteen to twenty percent of the prospects you call on are ecstatic with their present marketing campaign. No matter what you do or what you offer, you will not land these accounts.

Sixty percent of the prospects you contact, although they may claim to be happy with their campaign, are merely content; they are in a comfort zone. The campaign seems to be reaching the right readership, the CPM seems reasonable and the response seems adequate. But this 60% is open to suggestions and if offered better solutions to their marketing challenges, they will consider changing their campaign.

The remaining 15% to 20% of prospects you contact are totally dissatisfied with their present advertising and marketing results. These prospects are looking for alternative ideas.

So at any given moment, 75 - 80% of the prospects you contact will consider placing an ad in your publication.

# Make prospecting a habit

Not to undermine the importance of developing powerful selling skills that overcome objections and make closing easy, but in the overall scheme of things, nothing is more important than prospecting. After all, if you're not making a presentation you can't land a new account.

Furthermore, there is a direct correlation between the calls you make today and the income you'll earn tomorrow, so you must make prospecting a habit; you must prospect every day.

# The prospecting Tipping Point

If you were to take a cup of water that is presently at 60° F and increased the temperature, here is what you would observe. A 100% increase in heat energy would raise the temperature to 120° F but there would be no noticeable change to the water. A 200% increase in heat would raise the temperature to 180° F but still you would not notice any change. If you increased the heat by an additional 31°, bringing the temperature to 211° F you would still see no noticeable change in the water, so it would be easy to conclude that heat has little effect on water. But if you were to raise the temperature of the water by one additional degree you would hit the Tipping Point and notice a dramatic affect as the water starts to boil. The Tipping Point is where a small, seemingly insignificant action has a huge impact on results.

Tipping Points can be identified throughout the sales process and one of the most profound Tipping Points can be found in prospecting.

Accepted sales theory states that the more you prospect the more you'll sell, when in fact this theory does not hold true. For example, if you are presently calling on 2 new prospects each week but decided to increase your prospecting efforts and started calling on 6, 7, 8 or even 9 new prospects a week, you would expect that your hard work would result in a proportional increase in sales, when in fact you would notice little or no increase. But had you increased your prospecting activity from 9 new prospects a week to 10, you would have noticed a dramatic increase in sales because **10 new prospects** is the Tipping Point where prospecting activity starts to bring results.

Although there are numerous reasons why 10 is the prospecting Tipping Point there is a mathematical explanation for this phenomenon. If your closing rate is 10%, then meeting with less than 10 new contacts will bring zero results. So if you want to maximize your prospecting efforts; if you want to fast track your sales, the Tipping Point tells you that you must call on 10 new prospects a week.

# Always prospect at the top

When contacting a new prospect always start at the top of the corporate ladder.

Here are three reasons why prospecting at the top is absolutely vital.

1. A lower-level employee could block you from meeting with the real decision maker. For example, if your first meeting is with an administrative assistant or a buyer, it's extremely difficult to go over this individuals head and call on the marketing manager without stepping on toes.
2. Many employees have the authority to say *"No, we're not interested"* but few can say *"Yes."*
3. Only the president or owner has control over the budget.

If based on your previous experience, you know that the decision maker is the marketing manager you can ask for him or her by title, but if in doubt as to who to ask for, always start at the top of the corporate ladder.

# Call on large accounts

It takes no more effort to call on a large account than it does to call on a small business. In fact, in most cases, larger accounts are easier to land than small ones.

In a small company, where you are dealing with the owner, any expenditure affects him directly and therefore requires his careful consideration. So it's not unusual to make five or six calls to get a single ¼ page insertion. But when dealing with a larger corporation, management is not emotionally affected by capital expenditure; in fact they want to spend their budget. So if they like what you have to offer, they will instantly authorize the campaign.

Another reason that you must call on large accounts is because your income is more affected by the size of your clients than by the number of clients that you have.

# Never tell the receptionist what you are selling

Imagine it's evening and you are relaxing at home watching television or reading a good book. The telephone rings, you pick it up and this is what you hear,

*"Good evening, it's Peter from Best CARPET CLEANING. How are you tonight?"*

How would you respond to this call? Most of us would respond with three words, *"I'm not interested"*. But why would you be so negative? You haven't even heard my offer. I was about to tell you that as a promotion, a local radio station and a carpet manufacturer have selected your home to receive free wall to wall carpeting. This top-of-the-line broadloom is yours at no cost and even includes installation. You have nothing to buy.

The reason I didn't get a chance to tell you about my great offer is because the moment that you heard the words "carpet cleaning", you prejudged the value of my call and instantly decided that you were not interested.

It is no different when you are selling advertising. For example, when prospecting for new business never say,

*"Good morning, it's Peter from Best <u>Publishing</u>"* or

*"Good morning, we're the* publishers *of On Target* Magazine. *Can you please tell me who handles your* *advertising?"*

The moment the receptionist hears give-away words like publishing, advertising, media kit or magazine she will instantly prejudge the value of your services and she'll often say *"Thanks, but we're not interested".*

You must deny the receptionist the opportunity to screen your call, by dropping these give-away words or using an acronym. So instead of saying *"On Target Magazine"* you could say, *"Good morning it's "Peter from OTM ..."* or better still don't even mention a company name. Just say *"Good morning it's Peter ..."*

By implementing this small change you will instantly double the number of decision makers you'll get to talk to.

# Don't leave your telephone number

When you're prospecting a new account and you have not yet reached the decision maker, never leave your telephone number.

Leaving your telephone number is no different than leaving your company name. If the prospect returns your call and your receptionist answers the phone with *"On Target Magazine"* he'll know what you are selling and he'll prejudge the value of your services. Not only will he most likely hang up, but when you try to contact him again, he'll avoid your call.

When calling on a new account and the receptionist says *"I'm sorry but Ms Decision Maker is in a meeting, can she call you back?"* don't leave your telephone number. Instead say *"That would be great, but unfortunately she won't be able to reach me at this time, so I'll try her back a little later. When do you expect her to be free?"*

# Stop selling advertising

Here's an example of a standard telephone pitch that most salespeople use when calling on a new account.

*Mr. Prospect, it's Peter from Best Publishing. Thank you for taking my call. We publish On Target Magazine which is distributed to over 15,000 independent travel agents. The reason I'm calling is I'd like to have a few minutes of your time to quickly tell you about our marketing services and to show you some of the advantages of advertising in our publication.*

Although this pitch may sound good, it's missing the mark. Your prospects are not interested in your publication nor are they interested in advertising. What they really want to know is how you can help them reach their business and marketing goals.

If you want prospecting to become an easy task, you need to stop selling advertising. Instead, pique your prospect's interest by offering a Universal benefit. (See "Universal Wants" page 54)

# Ask for 5 minutes of their time

Most marketing managers have very busy schedules and often the busiest are our best prospects. One of the main reasons they're hesitant to talk to salespeople is they fear they'll be wasting valuable time. They're concerned about committing themselves to listening to a lengthy presentation, only to discover, within the first few minutes, that they're not interested. They are reluctant to commit their valuable time without an easy escape route, so always remove their fear by ensuring your prospects that your meeting will only take 5 minutes of their time.

Even though both you and the prospect know that the meeting will likely take longer, by making this statement you have given the prospect permission to excuse himself if he doesn't find your presentation of value. Under this condition the prospect is much more likely to grant you an appointment.

# Focus on one vertical market

What are your prospects looking for? They're looking for solutions to their business and marketing challenges; they are not looking for advertising. They want to work with someone who can make suggestions and offer new ideas, preferably an expert in *their* industry and they'll gladly pay a premium to anyone who can increase their probability of success and reduce their risk of failure. They want to work with a specialist who understands *their* industry's unique problems.

So instead of randomly calling on everyone who would benefit from advertising in your publication, focus your selling efforts by calling on one industry at a time.

By calling on businesses in the same industry you will quickly become familiar with common industry trends and challenges, you'll learn to speak the industry jargon and you'll uncover their specialized advertising and marketing needs. In short, by talking their language you'll be perceived as the industry expert your prospects are looking for.

**Steps to success**
Select 3 niche markets and compile a prospecting list for each market.

# Dealing with receptionists that won't give you the decision maker's name

**1. Call before 9 a.m. at lunch or after 5 p.m.**
While most receptionists start work at 9 a.m. and end at 5 p.m. managers often start working at 8 a.m and are still in the office after 6 p.m. So call before or after regular working hours and usually there is no one there to screen your call.

**2. Ask for sales**
Phone any company and ask for sales and they'll put you through instantly. When a salesperson picks up the phone all you need to do is ask for their help. *Good morning, my name is Peter and I'm with Best Publishing. I'm in sales like you. Would you mind if I asked you a few brief questions?*

You'll find that most salespeople will tell you anything you'd like to know because they haven't been instructed to screen calls.

**3. Call accounts receivable**
If your target company doesn't have a sales department, ask for accounts receivable and the receptionist will usually transfer your call instantly. Once again, accounting has not been instructed to screen calls so they see nothing wrong with answering your questions.

# Dealing with voice mail

1. Never leave your office telephone number. If the prospect returns your call he'll likely discover what you are selling and he'll prejudge the need for your services.

2. If you decide to leave your name, leave only your first name and keep the prospect guessing as to who is calling. Remember the old saying "Curiosity killed the cat."

3. Don't leave your company name - not even an acronym. If the prospect doesn't recognize it, it will alert him to the fact that a sales call is being made and he may try to avoid further contact.

4. If you expect your prospects to return your call, you'll need to create a sense of urgency and pique their curiosity by telling them very little. Here's an example of a short voice mail message that encourages a call back.

   *Hi ___Ted___, it's ___Peter___, give me a quick call if you can. You can reach me for the next 15 minutes at ___(Leave your cell number)___.*

5. Many managers have two telephone lines. One line is designated as their voice mail and the other is a direct line they answer. So the next time you reach voice mail, dial the next or previous sequential number and you'll often reach your prospect's direct line.

6. The most effective way to deal with voice mail is to press "0" on your phone, which will take you back to the switchboard operator. Now ask to have your prospect paged. Since many managers leave their voice mail on 24/7, they tell their clients, friends and family to page me if you need me.

   Don't worry that your page might interrupt an important meeting, because your prospect won't mind being paged if you have something of value to offer him. On the other hand, if you don't have something of importance to say you shouldn't be calling him in the first place.

# Always close for the appointment

Even if you've made a strong, persuasive telephone presentation that piqued the prospect's interest don't expect your prospects to invite you to their office, because in most instances they won't, unless you ask for the appointment.

When asking for the appointment never say, *"What time would be convenient for you?"* because the answer to this question is most likely *"Never"*. Instead, stay in control of the sale by using the Alternative Choice Close.

The premise of this closing technique is to give the prospect a choice between two different times, not a choice as to whether or not to see you.

*Mr. Prospect, I can be at your office tomorrow morning at 9:00 or do you prefer Wednesday at 2:00?*

# Ask qualifying questions before meeting the prospect

Here's a simple way to set yourself apart from other salespeople. Instead of using your first visit, with a new prospect, as a probing session, qualify the prospect by phone and use your first visit to sell.

To motivate your prospect to answer your qualifying questions over the phone, you'll need to assure him that answering these questions is in *his* best interest. So after he has agreed to the appointment say,

*Mr. Prospect, I look forward to meeting you tomorrow and I'll bring along some information I know you will find valuable. So that I only bring that information best suited to your needs, let me ask you a few brief questions.*

Now don't wait for your prospect's response. Immediately begin asking probing questions.

# Don't confirm your appointment

Considering the fact that your prospects only remember about 10% of what you told them during your telephone presentation, chances are they'll only have a vague idea of what the scheduled meeting is about. Therefore your appointment won't be high on their priority list and should the prospect find himself, even slightly, busy when you call to confirm, he's likely to give you several reasons why he can't see you.

Unless your appointment is out of the way, don't phone to confirm. Confirming your appointment only gives the prospect an opportunity to cancel.

# Door to door canvassing

# Don't hand out your business card

When canvassing door to door, handing the receptionist your business card can be a fatal mistake. The first thing she'll do is read it and when she does she is likely to discover that you are selling advertising so she'll resist giving you the marketing manager's or president's name.

Keep your business cards in your pocket. Instead, approach the receptionist with paper and pen in hand and say,

*Good morning, could I please get your* ***fax number****? Thank you, and how do you spell your marketing manager's last name? And the first name is? Thank you, is he in?*

By asking for the fax number, you are breaking down the receptionist's resistance to giving out information. She realizes that you can't disturb the marketing manager by fax and she feels that she can always screen the fax when it arrives so giving you the contact's name becomes a harmless activity.

# Don't stand by the receptionist's desk

When you stand in front of a receptionist your body language is saying *"Is there any information that you'd like to know?"* and of course there is; she'd like enough information to screen you. So here's what to do instead. Once you've asked to see the decision maker *"Could you please tell Ted that it's Peter and that I need to ask him a brief question"* immediately turn around and walk to the farthest corner of the reception area. Now don't look back at the receptionist. If she wants to ask you questions, such as *"What company are you with? What is this about?* or *Do you have an appointment?"* she'll first need to get your attention. If she does call you, answer her question then immediately turn and walk away again.

You'll find that some receptionists will call you once, very few will call you twice and less than 1 in 25 will call you a third time. Instead, they'll do what is easiest and follow through with your request by paging the decision maker.

# When you just can't get the appointment

If you've tried everything, but you just can't break into a major account, here's an idea that will usually open previously locked doors.

Have your editor interview the key decision makers at the company and more often than not you'll get the business.

# Farm major accounts

Although you'll find that when using proven and tested prospecting techniques, landing a qualified appointment with a major account becomes an easy task, there will still be some prospects who, regardless of how hard you try, will say *"I'm not interested"* or *"No, I'm happy with my existing marketing campaign"* and you will not get the appointment.

One of the best-kept secrets of top income earners is that they don't give up on these accounts. Instead, they *farm* them. Here's what to do.

1. Create a chart; a farming list that holds 25 accounts.

2. When you get turned down by a major account, add this account to your farming chart. When I say major account, I'm describing the type of account that would have a major impact on your income.

3. Contact every prospect on your farming chart, by mail, phone or fax, once each and every month, but don't try to sell them advertising. Instead, contact them to keep them informed of changes that could affect their business.

Now don't expect farming to bring instant results, but after you've been farming your accounts for about six months you'll begin to see some changes.

Prospects that previously turned you down will start to place ads. Here's why farming works.

1. As I've already mentioned, at any given moment, only 20% of the prospects you contact are truly happy with their marketing campaign; sixty percent are satisfied, while 20% are dissatisfied. But this is not a static environment. A prospect that is ecstatic with marketing results today may well be totally dissatisfied with the campaign tomorrow. Also keep in mind that a marketing campaign that is bringing outstanding results has only one way to go - down. So farming puts you in position to catch the ball when the present campaign starts to fizzle.

2. Although your prospecting efforts may have been stopped by a marketing manager who won't give you the time of day, statistics show that up to 50% of an organization's staff will turn over every 18 months, and management changes on average once every two years. So while some of these negative prospects will be at the beginning of their employment cycles, just as many will be near the end.

3. Farming is relationship selling at its best. After six months, many of the prospects on your list will start to consider you a friend and once they trust and like you, they will start to work with you.

**Steps to success**
Create a list of 10 reasons to contact the prospect.

# Turning objections into sales

# The Pivotal Point

There are 2 types of selling skills, Passive and Active and a whopping 90% are Passive skills. Not to undermine their importance but a lack of Passive selling skills does not preclude failure. Even if you have no Passive selling skills what-so-ever you'll still land some accounts. The only difference is that they'll need to work 8 – 10 times harder than those individuals that have mastered these skills and your earnings will not be reflective of your hard work.

Passive selling skills are pro-active. They are incorporated into the sales presentation and they are designed to preempt and defuse the prospect's resistance, resulting in a higher closing rate and an increase in dollar sales. Here are just a few examples of Passive selling skills.

**Creating a sense of urgency**
If your presentation doesn't give the prospect a strong reason to order today, he won't and the likelihood of getting a commitment is highest at the end of the presentation and diminishes quickly thereafter.

**Call on the client**
One of the biggest mistakes ad salespeople make is calling on agencies and media buyers in the hope that these individuals will sell the benefits of the magazine to the client.

**Never tell the receptionist what you are selling**

As soon as the receptionist discovers that you are selling advertising she'll prejudge the value of your services and she'll screen the call.

In total there are well over 150 Passive selling skills and without question these skills are the key to ultimate success. But as I've already mentioned a lack of Passive skills doesn't mean that you can't sell. Even if you call on advertising agencies, tell the receptionist what you are selling and fail to create a sense of urgency you'll still have some success. But clients will be far and few between and since you'll lose more often than win you'll quickly become unmotivated, resulting in an escalating decline in performance.

Although you can land new clients without developing your Passive skills you must - and I stress the word must - master Active selling skills because without Active skills you are doomed to fail. Here's a common scenario that explains the difference between Passive and Active selling skills.

Slick, a seasoned ad sales executive is prospecting for new business. He contacts a new account and says *"Good morning. I'm with Best Magazine can you please tell me who handles the advertising for your company."* As you can tell Slick has neglected a Passive selling skill. When Slick said *"Best Magazine"* he told the receptionist what he was selling and gave her the opportunity to prejudge the value of his services. But even though Slick makes this same mistake during each and every cold call, because it is a Passive selling skill all is not lost. He'll get to meet with some marketing managers and eventually he'll bump into one that is unhappy with his marketing campaign. In fact, when using this prospecting approach, on average, about 30% of the receptionists will provide him the information he requested but 70% will respond with one of the following objections.

*We're not interested*
*Our advertising agency handles our advertising*
*Just mail me a media kit*
*Not now call back in 6 months"*
*We don't give out that information*

The moment the receptionist raises an objection the dynamics of the sale begins to change and Passive selling skills lose their effectiveness. Slick has hit a pivotal point in the sales process. He's now facing a make-it or break-it situation and only Active selling skills will save the sale. Slick has either learned how to overcome the receptionist's objections or he'll lose 70% of the time.

Active selling skills are reactive. They are pre-planned replies that only come into play when the prospect objects. Active skills are proven and tested responses that overcome the prospect's resistance.

As you already know objections are not exclusive to prospecting; they are scattered throughout the entire sales process. Even if you've made a powerful and persuasive presentation (Passive skill), when asked to commit to a schedule 80% of your prospect will say,

*Let me think it over and I'll get back to you*
*I want to look at a few other publications before I decide*
*Your CPM is too high* or
*I want to discuss this with my partner/ad agency first*

So here's the bottom line. Although you may land the odd job without Passive skills you are dead in the water if you don't master Active skills because sooner or later every sales presentations will reach the pivotal point, where the decision to commit to a campaign teeters upon your ability to overcome the prospect's resistance. In other words, your success is directly proportional to your ability to overcome common objections so don't leave this skill to chance.

# Learn to expect objections

Learn to accept the fact that irrespective of how great your presentation and irrespective of how much your prospect wants to place an ad in your magazine, 8 out of 10 times the prospect will raise an objection before giving his final okay.

Not only must you learn to expect an objection - objections are part of the selling process - you should learn to welcome them, because an objection is usually an indication that your prospect is interested and ready to buy.

# Never pause after answering an objection

Answering an objection is not a debate nor is it a test of wits, but when you pause after answering an objection you are indirectly asking your prospect *"What do you think of my answer?"* and you can bet your bottom dollar that the prospect will not say *"Well, obviously you were right and I was wrong."* Instead, he'll defend his position and raise another objection to prove his point.

So never pause after answering an objection. Instead, immediately continue with your presentation or ask a closing question.

# Objections show you where your presentation is weak

If you're hearing the same objections over and over again, your prospects are telling you that your presentation is weak.

For example, if your prospects are always saying *"Your CPM is too high"* they are telling you that your presentation did not justify the price. Likewise, if they are always saying *"Let me think about it and I'll get back to you"* they are saying that you have not given them a reason to order today. And if you are always hearing *"I'm happy with my current advertising campaign"* they are telling you that you have not given them a valid reason to change. So instead of waiting for these objections to occur, beat the prospect to the punch by addressing common objections in your presentation.

*Mr. Prospect, we have an 87% renewal rate not because our CPM is the lowest but rather because our clients have found that advertising in our publication brings the highest return.*

**Steps to success**
For the next few weeks keep track of every objection you hear. Then take the two most common objections and address them in your presentation and you'll find that these objections will be gone forever.

# 80% of first objections are false

The fact that 80% of all first objections are false tells us two things;

1. Don't throw in the towel just because your prospect objects, and
2. Don't waste your time handling first objections until you are satisfied that the objection is true.

One of the most effective techniques for handling a first objection is to avoid answering it. This approach has several advantages; it allows you to continue with the flow of your presentation and it gives you extra time to think of a response, but most importantly, if the prospect does not repeat the objection you have eliminated it altogether.

To avoid answering an objection just agree with the objection and then proceed with your presentation.

**I never make a decision without talking to my partner first**
*Mr. Prospect, I understand, you obviously value your partner's opinion.* Now continue with your presentation.

**We are happy with our existing magazine campaign**
*Mr. Prospect, I understand and I wouldn't ask you to change that campaign.* Now continue with your presentation.

# Agree, before addressing an objection

When your prospects object, don't turn the objection into a debate or a discussion because you'll never prove your prospects wrong. You can't openly argue with someone and expect them to buy from you. Instead, the first thing you must do before responding to any objection is, to lower your prospect's defenses by agreeing. Whenever possible begin your response by saying *"I understand."*

**This is too expensive**
*Mr. Prospect **I understand**, but putting price aside, is there any other reason that you wouldn't place an ad in our publication?*

**I'd like to look at some other publications first**
*Mr. Prospect **I understand**, because many of my clients did the same thing, but after comparing publications they found that we offered the best return on investment. Isn't that what you are really looking for?*

**I want to talk to my partner first**
*Mr. Prospect **I understand**, but to secure your place in the summer issue, I'll reserve your space immediately. In the meantime you can talk to your partner and should she not approve of your decision just give me a call next week and I'll cancel. Isn't that a good idea?*

# Use objections to close the sale

The Sifter Close is a powerful technique that can be used to uncover the real objection and to turn an objection into a sale.

The theme of this close is to sift out the real objection by using one of the following phrases.

*Mr. Prospect,* ***if it were not for***
*the price*
*your partner*
*your budget*
*would you give us the go-ahead today?*

or

*Mr. Prospect,* ***if you could***
*get this ad for less*
*find the budget*
*would you give us the go-ahead today?*

For example, you ask for the order and the prospect says *"I need to talk to my partner first."* Using the Sifter Close you would say,

*Mr. Prospect I understand, but* ***if it were not for your partner*** *would you give us the go-ahead today?* If he says *"No"* then this is not a true objection, but if he says *"Yes"* then he has agreed to buy, if you can get his partner's okay.

Here's another example. If your prospect says *"We don't have the budget"* you can use the Sifter Close to instantly tell if this is a true objection.

*Ms Prospect I understand, but* ***if you could*** *find the funds would you give us the go-ahead today?* Again, if she says *"No"* then budget is not the true objection, but if she says *"Yes"* then she has agreed to buy if you can arrange financing.

Here's one last example. Prospects have learned that an easy way to get rid of salespeople is to tell them that the price is too high, so the next time your prospect says *"I can run the same ad in your competitor's publication for $500 less"* use the Sifter Close to see if he's telling the truth and to close the sale.

*Mr. Prospect, I don't believe that we can, but* ***if I could*** *find a way to run your campaign for $500 less would you give us the go-ahead?* If he says *"No"* then price is not the true objection, but if he says *"Yes"* you have landed the account if you can match the price.

# Preplan and practice your responses

Most of the thousands of salespeople making presentations every day are relying on their own imagination and experience to answer objections. Although some of these responses are excellent, the overwhelming majorities are mediocre at best and many are completely ineffective. While trying your best is an admirable trait, when you consider that your income depends upon your ability to overcome common objections, trying your best is not good enough, especially since the most powerful and motivating responses to all objections are readily available for anyone to use.

Our studies have shown that salespeople that use carefully planned responses to objections close on average four times as many sales as those who use spontaneous responses.

# Never give up until you've responded to 3 objections

While having the ability to overcome one or two objections may result in a small increase in sales, you will still fall short of your true income potential.

Most orders will not occur until after you've addressed the third objection, so never give up until you've responded to 3 objections.

**Steps to success**
At the end of this section you'll find field-tested responses to common objections. Don't just read these responses, instead select the 5 objections you hear most often and during the next few weeks read, repeat and practice these responses until they become second nature.

# The Repeat Response

If the prospect raises an objection and you find yourself lost for words, the Repeat Response is a powerful technique that will circumvent the objection and place the pressure back on the prospect's shoulders.

The Repeat Response takes advantage of the fact that 80% of all first objections are false, so in most cases the prospect will find the objection difficult to justify. To use this technique, simply repeat the objection - with an inquisitive tone - in the form of a question.

Prospect: The price is too high.

Question: *The price is too high?*

Prospect: I want to think it over.

Question: *You want to think it over?*

After repeating the objection, don't say a word. Instead let the prospect try to rationalize his objection.

# Responses to common objections

For ready-to-use responses that overcome price objections see Handling Price

# Send me a media kit

*That's exactly what I would like to do, but to ensure that the information in the media kit is perfectly suited to your needs, I'll need 5 minutes of your time.*

*My experience has been that a media kit often raises more questions than it answers. Since I'm sure your time is valuable, why don't you invest 5 minutes and I'll quickly share some ideas that could;*

- *increase sales*
- *improve your bottom line*
- *help you gain market share*

*When someone asks me to send a media kit it's usually for one of two reasons. They are either very interested in what we have to offer or they are just trying to get rid of me. If you don't mind me asking, which of the two possibilities are you in?*

*Reading a detailed media kit will not only take more of your time it will be much less informative and a lot less interesting than talking to me. Let me assure you I'll only need 5 minutes of your time to share some ideas that could;*

- *increase sales*
- *improve your bottom line*
- *help you gain market share.*

# I'm happy with my current advertising campaign

*That's exactly what many of my clients said before placing an ad in our publication. But after measuring response they discovered that our publication brought a much higher return on investment. Isn't that what you are really looking for?*

*I would never ask you to switch publications. All I'm looking for is 5 minutes of your time to quickly share some ideas that other companies like yours, are already using to increase sales and gain market share.*

*Every time I talk to a new customer they tell me that they are happy with their current advertising campaign. We have over 200 clients who are not happy, but rather ecstatic with the return on investment that they are getting from our publication. Which would you rather be happy or ecstatic?*

*The real question is. "What do we have to offer that you can't get from your present advertising campaign?" am I correct?*

*Just suppose that I could share some ideas that other companies like yours, are already using to increase sales, generate leads and gain market share. If that were the case you'd be interested, wouldn't you?*

# I'm not interested

*May I ask why you feel that you would not benefit from our marketing services?*

*Would you mind if I ask why you're not interested?*

*Obviously you have a good reason for saying that. Do you mind if I ask what it is?*

*I'm really surprised to hear that. Why wouldn't you want to examine some ideas that are already helping companies like yours gain a competitive edge?*

*Many of my clients felt the same way before they saw what we had to offer. All I require is 5 minutes of your time and I'll quickly share some ideas that other businesses like yours are already using to improve their bottom line.*

*I wouldn't expect you to be interested until you saw how my recommendations could increase your sales and improve your bottom line. Let me assure you this will only take 5 minutes.*

*Let me assure you that I'm not trying to sell you anything at this time. All I'm looking for is 5 minutes of your time so that I can quickly share some ideas that could increase your sales and profits. If you find these ideas as beneficial as I believe them to be, we can set up a future appointment.*

*All I ask for is 5 minutes of your time to quickly share some ideas that many of your competitors are already using to gain market share. In that way you can evaluate the benefits for yourself. Isn't that a good idea?*

*I rarely hear that. May I ask why you would not be interested in an idea that would increase your sales and improve brand recognition?*

*I truly believe that my recommendations are in your best interest and I thought that you felt the same way, but it seems that I was wrong. Do you mind if I ask why you are not interested?*

*If what you're saying is that you're not interested at this moment, I understand, but if you're saying that you're not interested at all, I'm a little confused. After all, why won't you want to look at some proven and tested ideas that could;*

- *increase your sales*
- *help you gain market share*
- *improve your bottom line*
- *generate leads*

*That's good, because I'm not looking for people that are interested. All I'm asking for is 5 minutes of your time to quickly share some ideas that other companies like yours are already using to increase sales and generate leads.*

# I'm too busy
# Call me in 6 months

*If you don't mind me asking, what are you hoping to gain by waiting?*

*What do you believe will be different in 6 months from today?*

*Just suppose that I could show you how to;*

- *increase sales*
- *gain market share*
- *improve your bottom line*
- *generate leads*

*If that were the case you wouldn't wait 6 months would you?*

*I can appreciate your hesitation but let me quickly reiterate the benefits of going ahead and remind you of the risk of delaying.*

With an astonished tone say *Why would you want to delay an opportunity that could;*

- *increase your sale*
- *improve your bottom line*
- *grow your market share*
- *give you a competitive edge?*

*No problem. I'll call back some other time when you are not as busy. But, so that you can decide whether or not to take my call, I'll just take 5 minutes of your time to briefly outline our services.*

*I understand and I certainly wouldn't waste your time nor mine if I didn't truly believe that my ideas could improve your bottom line.*

If the prospect's reason for not wanting to talk to you is that he's too busy, this response will circumvent his objection.

*That's okay; I don't need to meet with you at this time. I can get all the information I need from your assistant and then provide you with a detailed report that could increase sales and help you gain market share. What's your assistant's name?*

# I don't have time to listen to your presentation

Here's the situation. The prospect says *"I don't have time to meet with you so just give me the rate."*

You must avoid giving him a rate. He's price shopping and he'll most likely make a decision based on CPM.

*I'd be happy to give you a price but to ensure that you are getting the lowest price let me ask you a few brief questions.*

*You're not making this decision strictly based on price are you?*

*I wouldn't be doing my job if I simply gave you a price so I'd rather back away from this for now and re-address it when you have more time.*

# Our agency handles the advertising

*I would never ask you to change that policy. All I'm looking for is 5 minutes of your time to quickly share some ideas that other owners are already using to increase sales and improve their bottom line.*

*I'm not calling to sell advertising. All I'm looking for is 5 minutes of your time to share some ideas that other companies like yours are already using to increase sales and to gain market share. If you find them as beneficial as I believe them to be, we can set up a future appointment.*

*If I were selling adverting I'd be happy to call on them, but that's not what I do. I work with companies like yours offering solutions that;*

- *increase sales*
- *gain market share*
- *improve the bottom line*
- *generate leads*

*All I'm looking for is 5 minutes of your time to quickly share some ideas.*

# We are under contract

*I would never ask you to break a contract. All I'm looking for is 5 minutes of your time to quickly share some ideas that other owners are already using to increase sales and improve their bottom line.*

*I'm glad to hear that because this gives me time to work on some ideas that could;*

- *increase your sales*
- *help you gain market share*
- *improve your bottom line*
- *generate leads*

*All I need is 5 minutes of your time to ensure that there is a fit.*

# Don't need to advertise. We use trade shows

*I would never suggest that you stop using trade shows. All I'm looking for is 5 minutes of your time to share some ideas that other businesses like yours, are already using to increase sales and profits.*

*That's exactly why we should meet. I can quickly share some ideas that other companies, like yours are already using to enhance branding and increase attendance at their trade show booth.*

*The real question is "Will my ideas result in a high return on investment". That is the real question isn't it?*

*A number of my clients said exactly the same thing before taking advantage of our services. But after measuring response they discovered that our publication brought the best return on investment. Isn't that what you are looking for?*

# Our dealers do all our advertising

*I would never suggest that you change that policy. All I'm looking for is 5 minutes of your time to share some ideas that other businesses like yours, are already using to increase sales and profits.*

*Just suppose that taking advantage of my ideas resulted in a large increase in sales and profits. You'd want to know about of this opportunity wouldn't you?*

*That's exactly why we should meet. I can quickly share some ideas that other companies, like yours, are already using to drive sales through their dealers.*

Consider contacting the dealers and show them how inexpensive it would be to run a co-op ad.

*A number of my clients rely on their dealers for sales and marketing. Would you mind if I contacted them directly and shared some ideas that could increase sales*? (If he likes the idea ask him for a dealer list.)

*Do your dealers have the opportunity to earn co-op dollars?* (If *"Yes"* see "Selling co-op ads" page 37)

# Business is slow

*That's exactly why you should take a quick look at my suggestions. I can share some ideas that other companies, like yours, are already using to increase sales and profits.*

*Just suppose that I could show you how to;*

- *increase sales*
- *generate leads*
- *improve your bottom line*
- *gain market share*

*If that were the case you'd want to know about these ideas, wouldn't you?*

*Many of my clients have also mentioned that business is slow, in fact we've been able to help them increase sales and gain market share during these difficult times.*

*All I'm asking is that you evaluate some ideas that other companies like yours, are already using to turn things around. Let me assure you it will only take 5 minutes of your time.*

*Let me assure you that I'm not calling to sell you anything at this time. All I ask for is 5 minutes of your time to share some ideas that other companies like yours, are already using to increase sales and gain a competitive edge.*

# We use a sales force

*That's exactly why we should meet. I can quickly share some ideas that other companies like yours, are already using to generate high quality leads for their salespeople.*

*That's exactly why you should consider using our services. I can show you how to generate a continuous flow of qualified leads for your sales team; which will result in more sales and higher profits.*

*Just suppose that I could show you a cost effective way to generate quality leads and increasing sales while enhancing brand recognition. You'd want to know about this opportunity wouldn't you?*

*All I'm looking for is 5 minutes of your time to quickly share some ideas that other companies like yours, are already using to;*

- *increase sales*
- *generate leads*
- *improve their bottom line*
- *gain market share*

# Magazine advertising doesn't pay off

*You're absolutely right. In many cases running a magazine ad will not pay and if you wanted to run a single ad I would do my best to dissuade you from making this decision. But a well planned campaign, placed in the right publication, can bring a huge return on investment. And the proof to this claim lies in the fact that 87% of our clients renew or increase the size of their ads each year.*

(Also see "Dealing with skepticism" pages 88 -90)

# I want to look at some other publications first

*May I ask what you are hoping to find elsewhere that we don't offer here?*

*You must have a reason for wanting to shop around; may I ask what that reason is?*

*I thought our publication was perfectly suited to your needs yet you seem hesitant. May I ask what you are still unsure of?*

*It sounds to me that there are still some issues that you are concerned about. What would they be?*

*Many of my clients have the same policy. They also looked at other publications before making a final decision. But to guarantee your position in the June issue I'll reserve your space immediately. In the meantime you can shop around and should you change your mind, just give me a call next week and I'll cancel. It's a simple way of protecting your interests. Isn't that a good idea?*

*That's a good idea. In fact, I've made it my job to fully understand what all of my competitors have to offer. So what is it that you need to know in order to make this decision?*

*I want your business, but I also want your trust so that I might get your future business as well. The only way that you can be absolutely certain that you are getting the best return on your investment is by shopping around so I have done it for you.* (Now tell him about your competitors and why 100's of clients have found that your publication is the best choice.)

More often than not, the prospect that uses this objection has already decided on exactly what he wants. He's just shopping for a better price.

*Correct me if I'm wrong, but what you're really shopping for is to see if you can get this same campaign for less. Am I right?*

*I understand how you feel, it certainly doesn't hurt to be thrifty and many of my clients felt exactly the same way. But after shopping around they found that we offered the best value for their investment. Isn't that what you are looking for?*

(See "Dealing with price objections" page191)

# Let me think it over

*Is there anything that you are still unsure about?*

*What information do you feel will become available at a later date that isn't available now?*

*Would you elaborate for me? What is it that you really want to think about?*

*I'm certain that this campaign is perfectly suited to your needs and I thought that you felt the same way. Yet, you seem hesitant. May I ask what your concern is?*

*Oh, there must be something I have not yet adequately clarified. If you just tell me what it is I'd be happy to cover it more thoroughly.*

*That's no problem; can you tell me what your thoughts are so far so I can tell if there is some information I've left out of my presentation?*

*I'm glad to hear that you want to think about this, because you obviously wouldn't waste your time thinking it over if you were not interested. But as you know, the best time to make an accurate decision is while the facts are still fresh in your mind. So why don't we take a minute to review this together, just to make certain that you arrive at the right decision. Which is what you want, isn't it?*

*I understand because there's a lot to think about. But to guarantee your position in the May issue, I'll reserve your space immediately. In the meantime, you can think it over and if for any reason you change your mind just give me a call next week and I'll cancel. It's a simple way of protecting your interests. Isn't that a good idea?*

*What you really want to think about is the price, isn't it?*
If the prospect says *"Yes"* handle this as a price objection. If the prospect says *"No"* dig deeper.
*As a courtesy to me, could you tell me the real reason you are hesitant to go-ahead with this program today?*

# I want to discuss this with my partner

*I understand that you value your partner's opinion, but if it were not for your partner would you go-ahead with this program today?* If he says *"Yes"* the objection is true and he has agreed to run the ad subject to his partner's approval. If he says *"No"* ask him why he is unsure. His answer will reveal his real objection or concern.

*In your experience, dealing with your partner, is he likely to go for this campaign? Why or why not?*

*I'm certain your partner will have many questions that only I can answer. Can I reach him at this office?*

*To guarantee your position in the May issue, I'll write up the insertion order conditional upon your partner's approval.*

*I understand because many of my clients also discuss matters with their partner before making a final decision. But to guarantee your position in the May issue, I'll reserved your space immediately. In the meantime, you can discuss this with your partner and if for any reason he does not agree with your decision just give me a call next week and I'll cancel. It's a simple way of protecting your interests. Isn't that a good idea?*

# We've decided to hold off until the fall

Here's the scenario. You've made a presentation and asked for the order but instead of giving you the go-ahead, the prospect says *"We've decided to hold off with this until the fall."*

There's no reason to believe that the prospect has decided not to run the ad so just assume that he wants to go-ahead.

*That's absolutely no problem. To guarantee your position in the fall issue I'll write up the insertion order right now.*

*I'm pleased to hear that you've decided to go-ahead with this so I'll reserve your space in the fall issue immediately.*

# Handling price

We recently conducted a survey to identify exactly what prospects are looking for when selecting a magazine. First we contacted 134 magazine salespeople. Since they're out there on the frontline, they should have a pretty good idea of what their clients want. Our survey asked them *"When trying to land a new account, what are most decision makers looking for?"* A startling 84% of the salespeople indicated that their prospect's foremost concern was getting the lowest CPM.

Needless to say we wanted to confirm the salespeople's response so we contacted 85 advertisers and asked them a similar question *"What do you look for when buying magazine ad space?"* Fortunately, their response was entirely different from that of the salespeople. Not to say that they were not concerned about the price, but contrary to what the salespeople said, 91% of the decision makers said they would pay extra to list in a publication that had higher readership and offered a potentially better return on investment. Only 9% indicated that CPM was their primary concern.

Although our survey clearly explained why so many salespeople are having difficulty selling ads - they're selling price to prospects who want sales, leads and branding - the responses begged another question. *"Why do so many salespeople believe that price dominates their prospects' buying decision?"*

The answer to this question is; most prospects do base their buying decision on CPM. Not because that's what they want, but rather because most salespeople force this decision by sending a media kit and rate card.

When selling face to face, CPM counts for less than 20% in the decision-making process, so your prospects are easily influenced by a strong presentation that justifies a higher price. But when the prospect is sitting alone at his desk comparing rate cards, his buying decision becomes dominated by price. After all, when each publication seems to be reaching the same market, why shouldn't he choose the one with the lowest CPM?

# Don't be afraid to quote the highest CPM

Does the lowest price usually win?
If people were truly as price conscious as they claimed Mercedes and Cadillac would be out of business and Lada would be the bestselling car in the country.

Although your prospects want a fair and competitive price, they will pay more if your presentation shows them that your publication has more to offer. In fact, studies have shown that price accounts for only 20% in the decision-making process. So don't be afraid of quote the highest CPM as long as it is supported by a strong presentation that justifies your price. (See "Focus on ROI instead of CPM" page 91)

# Sell a complete marketing solution instead of an ad

Offering a complete marketing solution is the most effective way to eliminate the CPM challenge.

Consider this common scenario. The prospect says *"What's the price for a ¼ page, black and white ad, to be placed in 6 issues?"* and you give her a quote. As you try to close the sale she reaches into her desk and produces a competitor's rate card and says *"Look, I can run the* ***same*** *ad in this publication for considerably less."* How would you respond? How could you justify your higher CPM?

You could talk about your higher readership and superior editorial content, but because you quoted her exact specs, you're now facing an up-hill battle. Fortunately, this situation is totally avoidable. Since your prospect can only compare apples to apples, all you need to do is submit an orange. In other words, instead of selling an ad use the Ad Shuffle to sell a multi-tiered marketing solution. (See "The Ad Shuffle" page 186)

# Highlight all changes

Here's how your prospect will read your proposal. First he'll look to see who the proposal was submitted by and then he'll proceed to the end of the proposal to look for the price. If your price is substantially higher than the other quotes, he'll most likely dismiss your proposal from further consideration, irrespective of the fact that your proposal may well have much more to offer.

For example, your proposal might include a free bonus mailing, a listing in the annual buyer's or show guide, or a banner ad on your website, but keep in mind that your prospect will not search your proposal for additional benefits. It's your responsibility to draw your prospect's attention to any benefits that would justify your higher price, by highlighting them with a bright yellow marker.

Likewise, if you've made a change that lowers the price, you must also draw this change to your prospect's attention otherwise the prospect may feel that you are trying to pull the wool over his or her eyes. For example, if the prospect asks you to quote a ½ page, 4 color ad, but you feel it is in your prospect's best interest to run a ½ page, 2 color ad, you must draw this change to your prospect's attention by highlighting the change.

# Never mail or fax your proposal

Unless you are submitting a quote to an existing customer, never mail, email, fax or drop off your proposal.

Your proposal cannot make a presentation; it will not justify your CPM and it cannot respond to objections, address concerns or close - only you can do that. So always present your proposal in person.

There are some situations in which you cannot deliver the proposal in person - the prospect's office may be too far away or the prospect might refuse to see you - but even so forwarding the proposal is a costly mistake because once the prospect has your quote he no longer needs to talk to you. So here's how to present the proposal to a **remote prospect**.

- Contact the prospect and setup a time and date for a 5 minute conference call.
- Just before the conference call, fax a copy of the proposal to the prospect's assistant and ask the assistant to deliver the proposal to the prospect. Make sure that the proposal **does not include the price.**
- When you call the prospect make a complete presentation that justifies your price and outlines the benefits; **only then mention the price and close**.

# Don't pause after stating the price

Here's how most of us deliver the price. At the end of the presentation we say "*Mr. Prospect, your total investment is only $1,500 per issue*" and then we pause and silently wait for the prospect to say *"I'll take it."*

When you pause after stating the price you are indirectly asking the prospect the question *"What do you think about the price?"* and you can be certain that the answer will not be *"It's too cheap."* Instead, you'll most likely face a price objection; an objection that is purely the result of poor presentation skills.

Many price objections can be avoided by following this simple rule: never pause after stating the price. Instead, ask a closing question or immediately continue with your presentation. If the price really is a problem, the prospect will bring it to your attention, but don't give him an open invitation to discuss the price. Make this small change and you'll find that price objections will become few and far between.

# Don't use the words price, cost or payment

We've all been conditioned to believe that the price is too high, that things cost too much and that we should try to reduce our payments, so don't use these negative words. Instead, use only the word *investment* when talking about the price.

*Ms Prospect, your total **investment** is only $2,500 per issue. Now, did you want to receive some extra copies of the magazine each month or is one copy enough?*

# Always sell the unit price

One of the fundamental rules, when dealing with price, is that you must make the price sound affordable and easy to accept.

For example, to run a ½ page ad in 12 issues, may costs $2,500 per issue, but if the publication's circulation is 18,000, the investment is only 14 cents per ad.

Unit price per ad = $\frac{\text{Cost of ad}}{\text{Circulation}}$

If you include secondary readership, the investment is only 7 cents per prospect.

Unit price per prospect = $\frac{\text{Cost of ad}}{\text{Total readership}}$

It's a lot easier to sell the benefits of investing 14 cents per ad or 7 cents to reach a potential customer than it is to sell $2,500 per issue.

So when making a presentation always focus on the unit price. Also mark it on your proposal and don't forget to highlight it.

# Use the Price Difference Close to justify a higher price

The Price Difference Close is a powerful technique that you can use to make a higher price seem more affordable.

**Up-selling to a larger ad**

You've quoted $3,500 for a full page ad and the prospect says *"That's too expensive. I don't want to spend more than $2,500 so I think we'll go with a half page."*

Most of us will now revert to our presentation and try to justify the $3,500 investment, when in fact we should be justifying only the price difference.

| | |
|---|---|
| $3,500 | Your price |
| $2,500 | What the prospect is willing to spend |
| $1,000 | **Price difference** |

**Unit Price Difference** = **Price difference** / Total readership

Don't forget that total readership is circulation, plus secondary or pass along readership, so for a 15,000 circulation, total readership could easily be 30,000 or more.

Unit Price Difference = $1,000 / 30,000

= 3 cents per customer

Now show the prospect the benefits he will gain by investing an additional 3 cents.

- Additional exposure
- Increased readership
- Enhanced credibility
- Higher response

**Up-selling color**

The prospect is interested in running a black and white ad but after reviewing his marketing objectives you feel that it is in his best interest to run the ad in full color.

| | | |
|---|---|---|
| Full color ad | $4,000 | |
| Black and white ad | $2,800 | |
| | $1,200 | Price difference |

**Unit Price Difference** = **Price difference** / Total readership

= $1,200 / 30,000

= 4 cents per prospect

Now show the prospect the benefits he will gain by investing an additional 4 cents.

**Selling against a low priced competitor**

| | | |
|---|---|---|
| Your price | $3,000 | |
| Their price | $2,000 | |
| | $1,000 | Price difference |

$$\textbf{Unit Price Difference} = \frac{\textbf{Price difference}}{\text{Total readership}}$$

$$= \frac{\$1{,}000}{30{,}000}$$

$$= 3 \text{ cents per prospect}$$

Now show the prospect the benefits he will gain by investing an additional 3 cents.

- Better qualified decision makers
- Better editorials
- Higher readership
- Higher response

# When the prospect asks for a discount, never pause

When your prospect asks for a discount, a simple *"No"* will usually dissuade the prospect from pursuing the matter any further. But even the slightest pause or hesitation after a discount request tells the prospect that you are thinking about it, and that means *"Yes"*.

So when your prospect says *"Can I get a discount?"* never pause. Immediately respond with *I'm sorry but we don't give discounts. I believe in giving my clients the best price right from the start. Isn't that a better policy?*

# Always get a commitment before offering a discount

Here's a common scenario. The prospect says *"I'm interested, but if I'm going to consider a 6 month schedule I need an additional discount"* and the salesperson responds by saying *"I don't think we can offer a further discount but let me talk to my manager to see what we can do"*. Confident that he'll land the account, he calls back on the prospect and says *"Mr. Prospect, you'll be pleased to hear that I was able to get you an additional 10% discount"* but instead of agreeing to the schedule the prospect says *"Great, but I still think your price is too high."* Fortunately, you can totally avoid this situation by following this important rule; find out how much of a discount the prospect is hoping to get and always get a commitment before offering a discount.

*Mr. Prospect, I don't believe my manager will approve a 10% discount, but we can certainly write up the insertion order and try.*

*Mr. Prospect, I don't believe that my manager will approve a 10% discount, but if he did would you give us the go-ahead?*

If he refuses to write up the order or to give you the go-ahead, don't waste your time trying to arrange a discount - it's not the real objection. But if he says "*Yes*" he has given you his commitment to buy.

# Responses to discount requests

*The only publishers that offer discounts are those that initially charge too much. We pride ourselves in offering all our clients the best service at the best price right from the start. Now isn't that a better policy?*

*It is our company policy to ensure that all our clients get a fair and competitive price. Giving discounts would not only require us to shortcut our services, but it would be unfair to those customers who did not receive it. Wouldn't you agree?*

*Our reputation has grown not because we are the cheapest, nor are we the most expensive, but because our clients have learned that advertising with us gives them the best value for their investment. Isn't that what you are looking for?*

*I've spent many years selling advertising and during that time I've worked for publishers with a variety of different pricing policies. Some would inflate their prices and then offer as much as a 40% discount - but only to those customers that fought hard enough and even then they often paid too much. I believe in giving all my clients the best price right from the start. Isn't that a better policy?*

*How much faith would you have in a doctor who offered a discount to get your business? Like other professionals we don't give discounts but we do give away ideas that could improve your bottom line. Isn't that what you really want?*

*I'm so glad you asked. If you were to run your ad in 12 issues, I could offer you a 15% discount. Would you like to take advantage of this discount or should I just mark you down for 6 issues?*

*I can't offer you a 10% discount but I might be able to;*

- *upgrade your ad*
- *including a free banner*
- *include your listing in the buyer's guide*
- *offer free positioning*

# The Ad Shuffle

Imagine for a moment that you are looking to buy a new house. You phone Clone Real Estate and their agent shows you a house in a subdivision full of identical model homes. Each house in the subdivision is built on an identical lot and is located on the same street. The only difference between these homes is that the price varies and the house your agent is trying to sell costs $30,000 more than the other homes in this subdivision. Would this real estate agent have difficulty selling this house? Of course he would; after all how can he justify the difference in price when everything is the same?

What if the more expensive house was built on a slightly different lot or if it was located on a different street? What if the more expensive house, although having the same square footage, was a different model? Could these differences be used to justify a higher price? The answer is obviously "Yes". A strong presentation could turn these differences into benefits that could make the expensive house a better investment.

Like Clone Real Estate, **you'll continue to lose sales to lower CPM as long as you continue to sell ads.** After all, why should anyone advertise with you if they can run the same ad elsewhere at a lower CPM. While you might be able to justify a slightly higher CPM by pointing out that you have better editorial content, a higher readership and a more targeted circulation, you'll still be fighting an up-hill battle.

Fortunately, there is a simple selling technique that allows you to consistently land the account even when yours is the highest CPM. The technique is called the Ad Shuffle and here's how it works.

Unless you are absolutely certain that your CPM is the lowest, stop selling ads and start selling multi-tiered marketing campaigns; *in other words always include a merchandising offer in your proposal*. For example, instead of pricing a ½ page ad - which the prospect can easily compare to the CPM in your competitor's publication - your proposal could include the cost of the ad campaign plus;

- A listing in your trade or product directory
- A direct mail, postcard campaign
- An 8 ½ x 11" insert in your magazine
- An email blast
- A banner ad on your website
- A product promotion
- A mailing list
- An advertorial
- A bonus magazine distribution
- A blow-in card
- A selective promotional mailing

To further differentiate your proposal you should also be looking for ways to change the ad. For example, you could change the size, offer premium positioning, remove or add color, quote multiple ads per issue or increase/decrease the length of the campaign. The important thing is that you **make your <u>campaign</u> different from the competition.**

Pricing a multi-tiered marketing campaign that includes a merchandising offer and changes to the ad, eliminates price competition, because these changes make it impossible for the prospect to accurately compare CPM and that allows you to make a presentation that justifies your higher price. But keep in mind that any changes you make must always be in the prospect's best interest.

**Steps to success**
On a sheet of paper list all the possible changes that can be made to an ad campaign and compare every proposal to this list.

# Don't share your ideas until they are ready to buy

You're meeting with a new prospect who is interested in placing a ½ page ad in 6 issues. After asking probing questions about the prospect's marketing and business objectives, you see a golden opportunity to increase the effectiveness of the campaign while showing the prospect that you know more about advertising than he does.

Salesperson: *Mr. Prospect, may I ask why you've decided to limit your marketing campaign to only 6 issues?*

Prospect: *That's all our budget will allow.*

Salesperson: *Mr. Prospect, studies have shown that frequency is the key to marketing success. May I suggest running a ¼ page ad in 12 issues instead of a ½ page ad in 6 issues and that you supplement your campaign by running a banner ad in our weekly e-newsletter? Let me explain how this will result in a higher response.*

In this all too common scenario, the salesperson did an excellent job of helping his prospect, but helping the prospect can be a costly mistake. If the prospect likes your new ideas he will ask other publications to price a 12 issue, ¼ page, plus banner ad campaign and you will have destroyed your competitive edge. All the quotes will once again be identical and price will become the only distinguishing feature.

When you see an opportunity to help your prospects - pique their interest by telling them what you can do - but never show your prospects how to enhance their marketing campaign until they are ready to buy.

Instead of sharing ideas, here's what to say at the end of your meeting.

*Mr. Prospect, based on what you've told me I can see several ways of increasing the effectiveness of your ad campaign. Would you mind if I* ***submitted*** *a few suggestions?*

Now that you've piqued the prospect's interest leave, and return with your suggestions and ideas when the prospect is ready to order.

# Dealing with price objections

# This is too expensive

*You're not making this decision strictly based on price are you?* (If *"No") May I ask what other factors you are taking into consideration?*

*I understand everything is so expensive these day. But putting price aside is there any other reason that you wouldn't take advantage of this opportunity to increase your sales and profits?*

*Is price your most important consideration?*

*Off the record Ted, what price were you thinking of?*

*Maybe it is, so let me ask you, how much were you hoping to spend?*

*Is price the only thing preventing you from going ahead with this campaign?*

*That's exactly what every one of my clients said before listing in our publication. But after measuring response, they discovered their return on investment far outweighed the cost. Isn't that what you are really looking for?*

*The real question is 'Does the return on investment justify the cost?' That is the real question, isn't it?*

*Which would you rather have price or profit? As you know you can't have both.* If he selects price he's most likely not a decision maker but rather a buyer.

*You could save money by running a smaller ad, but that would cost you readership and response. That's not what you are looking for, is it?*

*I understand that this costs slightly more than you planned on spending and if the price really is too high I can show you how to cut corners. Just let me know how much you want to invest and I'll adjust the ad accordingly. But you must understand that you will not draw the same readership and this will affect your marketing results.*

*I understand, but if price were not an issue would you go ahead with this?* If the prospect says *"Yes"* ask him *"Why?"* Now don't say another word, you must let the prospect respond because his answer will tell you exactly how to close.
If he says *"No"* ask him *"Why?"* His answer will reveal his real objection or underlying concerns.

One of the best ways to find out what's on the prospect's mind is to have him answer his own objection.
*What makes you say that?*
*What do you mean?*
*What are you comparing the price to?*

Use the "Price Difference Response" (see page 179) to show the client that he is only trying to save pennies per ad.

# This is $500 too expensive

*I don't believe that we can run your ad for $500 less, but if we could, would you give us the go-ahead?*

*I understand that this costs slightly more than you planned on spending and if the price really is too high I can show you how to cut corners. Just let me know how much you want to invest and I'll adjust the ad accordingly. But you must understand that you will not draw the same readership and this will affect your marketing results.*

Use the "Price Difference Response" (see page 179) to show the client that he is only trying to save pennies per ad.

*Mr. Prospect, I might be able to find a way to reduce the cost by 1.2 cents per ad, but that would mean cutting corners. You don't want to jeopardize the ad's effectiveness just to save a few cents do you?*

*What I hear you saying is that you need to justify investing that extra 2 cents per ad. So let me show you the additional benefits you are getting for those 2 cents.*

# This costs more than I thought

This is not an objection, it's a statement so don't try to overcome it. The prospect did not say that he was unwilling to go-ahead so all you need to do is acknowledge the comment and close the sale.

*I know what you mean; everything is so expensive these days. As you know, your ad in the November issue includes a free mailing list. Would you like this list sent to your attention or to someone else's?*

# I can place the same ad with a competitor for less

*Over 87% of our advertisers renew their ad, not because we are the cheapest but rather because our publication generates the best return on investment. Isn't that what you are looking for?*

*Of course some publishers will offer to run your ad for less. That's because our competitors know what their service is worth.*

*May I ask you a question? Does your company offer the lowest price on the market? Then we both agree that price is not the only consideration when making a purchase. In fact, the higher priced product may well offer better value, wouldn't you agree? So let me show you the extra benefits you'll get when advertising in our publication.*

*I know how you feel and many of my clients felt the same way. But after measuring response they found that our publication offered the best return on investment. Isn't that what you're really looking for?*

*I understand that price is important but in the overall scheme of things which is more important, the cost or the response you get from your ad?*

*If you could get the identical advertising campaign elsewhere for less, I wouldn't blame you for taking the offer. But although other publishers may offer to run your ad for less I'm not aware of any other publication that can offer the same return on investment.*

*The real question is 'Does the return on investment justify the advertising cost?' That is the real question, isn't it?*

*I've been in this business for over 8 years and I have not yet found a publisher that can offer the highest readership and the lowest prices; it's always a compromise. You don't want to jeopardize response just to save a few cents, do you?*

*When you buy a dress, a car or even a steak, you wouldn't automatically select the lowest priced item because you know that even a small difference could easily justify spending a little extra. The same holds true for advertising. Although you could run your ad in a publication that has lower readership and therefore charges less, this will affect your response, so let me explain why it's to your advantage to spend a few cents more.*

*As you know, you always get what you pay for, so our company decided that although investing in high quality editorials costs a little more, the resulting increases in readership far exceeds the small price difference.*

You can also use "The Ad Shuffle" technique to eliminate this objection. See page 186.

# He shows you a lower rate card

*I appreciate your honesty. Is price the only obstacle preventing you from going ahead with this?*

*I understand your concern but price aside, is there anything else preventing you from going ahead with this?*

*Is price the only thing that stands in our way?*

*I understand your concern, but wouldn't you agree that the success of this campaign will be measured in response and sales – not by what you spent. Let me show you how investing an extra 3 cents per ad will ensure you get the best response.*

*May I ask you a question? Does your company offer the lowest price on the market? Then we both agree that price is not the only consideration when making a decision. In fact, the higher priced product may well offer better value, wouldn't you agree? So let me show you the extra benefits you'll get when advertising with us.*

*We are not the cheapest nor are we the most expensive, but dollar for dollar our clients have found that we offer the best value for their investment. Isn't that what you are looking for?*

*What I hear you saying is that you need to justify investing that extra 2 cents per ad. So let me show you the additional benefits you are getting for those 2 cents.*

*I can certainly understand you taking great pains to compare rates. I'm curious, are you comparing identical rates? The reason I ask is; rate cards often have hidden costs. Do you mind if I take a quick look to ensure that the ad, circulation and readership are identical?*

*Of course some publishers will offer to run your ad for less. That's because our competitors know what their service is worth.*

You can also use "The Ad Shuffle" technique to prevent your prospects from comparing price. See page 186.

# Is there something you can do about the price?

This is not an objection but rather a question, so all you need to do is answer it. When your prospect says *"Is there anything you can do about the price?"* you must immediately respond, with *"I'm sorry but I believe in giving all my customers the best price right from the start. Isn't that a better policy?"* Even the slightest pause, tells the prospect that you are thinking it over and that means the price in negotiable.

Here's another response that will keep the sale moving forward.
*Mr. Prospect, of course I can do something about the price, but I wouldn't feel right charging you more.*

# No budget - funds frozen

*I understand, but if it were not for the lack of funds would you go-ahead with this campaign?*

*Just to make sure that I fully understand, are you saying that you would like to advertise in our publication but the price is over your budget or are you saying that you can't justify the investment?*

Before attempting to handle a budget objection you need to know;

1. The new budget date and
2. Amount of funds on hand

**New budget date**
Although the prospect many not have the funds at this time, he'll have the resource to make the purchase when he receives his new budget and that could be within the next few months. For example, if you know his new budget comes due in 90 days, you could; run his first ad 30 days before his new budget date or start the campaign immediately and extend his terms. So you must find out when the new budget comes into effect.

*Many of my clients are also having budget challenges; if you don't mind me asking, when does your new budget come into effect?*

**Funds on hand**

Just because the prospect says he doesn't have the budget, does not necessarily mean that he has no money. For example, if the campaign costs $12,000 but the prospect only has $6,000 in his budget, he might reject the campaign because of insufficient funds. Knowing about the funds on hand could allow you to save the sale. For example, you could take the $6,000; run the campaign and collect the balance when the new budget comes into effect.

*I understand your dilemma because many of my clients are in a similar position, but when you say that you don't have the budget are you saying that you have no funds on hand or insufficient funds to proceed with this campaign?*

**Responses to no funds**

*A client of mine faced a similar situation and had an interesting solution. Although she didn't have the budget, she was able to run the campaign by sharing the cost with a number of different departments. Isn't that a good idea?*

*You obviously understand the inner workings at your company so even though you don't have the budget to run this campaign, is there a budget in another department you could draw from?*

# Secrets of the master closer

# Selling the prospect is not enough

How much do you get paid for finding a new prospect?
How much do you earn for making a great presentation?
What do you get for helping your prospects with their marketing campaign?
How much of a bonus do you receive for overcoming an objection?

So far you haven't earned a cent, in fact selling the prospect on the benefits of magazine advertising is a complete waste of time and effort unless you follow through with the all-important step and close the sale. Remember, just because you've sold the prospect does not mean the prospect will order from you. He will buy from the salesperson that closes him.

# Closing only works if the prospect is already sold

Of the five selling skills; prospecting, presentation, overcoming objections, handling price and closing none is more misunderstood than closing. For years, closing gurus have been preaching the virtues of closing, leading us to believe that closing is almost magical, that this skill in-it-self has the power to dramatically increase our sales.

The truth is that even the best closing techniques are powerless. They can't persuade, motivate or entice a prospect to buy. In fact, the stories about the master closer who has the ability to pressure his prospects into buying, is nothing more than an old wives tale. For example, if I were to bring ten of the world's best closers together in one room, do you believe that these experts could use their finely honed closing skills to sell you a vacuum cleaner or a cellular phone if you didn't want these products? Of course not, because irrespective of how masterful they are in the art of closing, closing only works when the prospect is ready to buy. Let me stress this point again, closing only works when the prospect is ready to buy; but most sales trainers are reluctant to share this fact because it takes the hype out of their books and seminars.

The sale is made or lost in the presentation. If you've made a powerful presentation that solved the prospect's marketing problem, closing will be easy, but if you haven't made a great presentation, then all the closing techniques in the world won't convince the prospect to buy.

Although I've made closing seem somewhat trivial, let me assure you that developing your closing skills is vital to your success. In fact, nothing you do will have a greater, immediate impact on your sales than honing this skill. Here's why. People procrastinate; we're always putting things off until the last minute. Perhaps it's because our parents conditioned us to carefully think before we act or maybe it's just that we've been taken in the past so we don't want to be taken again. Whatever the reason, when it comes to making a buying decision, we stall. So don't expect anything different from your prospects.

Irrespective of how impressed they are with your presentation, when it comes to committing to the campaign most of them will say "*Let me think it over and I'll get back to you.*" Closing is the all important step that helps them overcome their procrastination and encourages them to act today.

# How to tell if the prospect is ready to buy

The Final Trial Close is a powerful technique that measures buying readiness. Here's how it works. At the end of your presentation, just before asking a closing question say,

*Ms Prospect, during the past 30 minutes I've made several recommendations that I believe are in your best interest and I think you feel the same way. Is there anything you are still uncertain about?*

or

*Ms Prospect, I've just shared a number of ideas I believe will increase your sales and help you gain market share. Is there anything you are still uncertain about?*

If she says *"No"* you are ready to close. On the other hand, if she says *"Yes, I do have a few questions"* then the prospect is not ready to buy, in which case closing would be a waste of time if not a terminal mistake, until after you've addressed her concerns.

# The closing Tipping Point

Throwing in the towel too early is one of the most costly mistakes that salespeople.

If you expect your prospects to immediately say *"I'll take it"* at the end of your presentation, you're in for many disappointments. Irrespective of how badly your prospects want to run an ad in your publication, eight out of 10 times they'll say *"Let me think it over and I'll get back to you"* so you must learn to expect these stalls and you must help your prospects overcome their indecision.

It is an undisputed fact that 80% of your prospects will not give you the okay until the third closing attempt. So always close three times.

# Preplan your closing questions

Closing is a critical part of the sale. It is where all your efforts - prospecting, qualifying, overcoming objections, presentation and quoting come together and the sale hangs in the balance. And it takes no more than a badly worded question to lead your prospect to say *"No"* and you walk away with nothing.

Remember, the words you use and how you say them make all the difference in how your prospect will react and the phrasing of your closing question will determine the response that you'll get, because people give responses that are appropriate to the questions being asked.

When you consider that all your efforts come down to the wording of one final closing question, it is imperative that you preplan and practice exactly what you will say.

# Get the order and leave

Imagine you have just completed a presentation to a major account and have succeeded in selling them a 2 page spread, to run in 6 issues. As the marketing manager fills out the paperwork, you continue to tell him about your great publication and during this conversation you say *"And as a bonus distribution, for the next 3 months the magazine will also be delivered to over 1,500 production managers."* As these words leave your mouth, the marketing manager stops writing and says *"I'm not interested in reaching production managers; they're not part of our target market."* Although you do your best to show him that this is a bonus distribution and that the regular distribution still reaches his market, he cancels the campaign.

While this example may be extreme, there is an important lesson to be learned here; after you've sold an ad, don't buy it back by telling your prospect too much. In other words, stop talking about the ad or the campaign because any additional information could turn the prospect off emotionally. Instead, thank him for the order and leave.

*Mr. Prospect, thank you for selecting our publication and let me assure you that you'll be extremely satisfied with the results.*

# Always close on a minor point

When you ask your prospect to buy ad space or commit to a campaign, you are asking him to make a major decision, so before giving his final okay the prospect will ask himself a number of questions.

- Will I get enough business from this campaign?
- Is this campaign worth the investment?
- Is this publication the right place to spend my advertising dollars?
- Do I need to decide now?
- Do I really need a full page ad?
- Should I commit to a 12 month schedule?
- Will my boss approve of my decision?

Unless the prospect can answer *"Yes"* to each and every one of these questions, he'll have no choice but to think it over before giving his final okay.

But you can avoid having your prospect make these major decisions by closing the sale on a minor point. For example, instead of asking your prospect to buy, you could say,

*Mr. Prospect, your ad will run in 12 consecutive issues starting in June and I'll send copies of each issue to your attention. How many copies would you like?*

Although a $25,000 ad campaign could be on the table, the decision to buy comes down to how many copies of each issue the prospect wants.

So never ask your prospects to give their approval on placing an ad; instead, get the go-ahead on a minor, insignificant part of the campaign and the rest of the campaign will follow.

# Never speak after asking a closing question

All too often a salesperson will ask a closing question such as *"Mr. Prospect, I will immediately reserve space for your ad in the June issue. Do you have a preference on positioning?"* and if the prospect doesn't immediately respond the salesperson will let him off the hook by saying something like *"As I've mentioned you'll be very satisfied with the results."*

Although those few seconds of silence, of dead air, may seem like hours, you must resist the temptation to speak. You must wait for your prospect to answer your closing question, because if you speak first you will destroy the closing attempt and your prospect will recognize your inability to keep silent.

Remember, after asking a closing question the first person to speak loses.

# The Alternative Choice Close

This is one of the oldest, yet still one of the most effective, closing techniques. The premise of this technique is to close the sale by asking your prospect to choose between two minor points. Never ask your prospect to consider a major point because major points require major decisions and your prospect will have no choice, but to think it over.

Here are some examples of The Alternative Choice Close. In each example the prospect agrees to buy by answering a simple question.

*Mr. Prospect, I have reserved space for your ad in the May, June and July issues. Did you want me to send a copy of each issue to your attention or to someone else?*

*Mr. Prospect, I have reserved space, so your ad will run in the next 6 issues. Did you want Reader Service information requests sent to you by email or fax?*

*Ms. Prospect, I will reserve space for your ad in the June issue immediately. Now would you prefer to have your ad placed on the right or left hand page?*

*Mr. Prospect, the artwork for your ad will be ready next week. Would you like to come to our office to review it or should I have it delivered?*

*Mr. Prospect, as you know, along with your ad in the April issue you'll receive an audited mailing list of 2,000 names and addresses. Would you like this list sent to your attention or to someone else?*

*Mr. Prospect, I have reserved space for your ad in the August and September issues. Will you be providing the artwork on disk or via email?*

*Ms. Prospect, I will immediately reserve space for your 12 month campaign. Should I send the layout specs to your attention or to your graphic artist?*

*Mr. Prospect, to maximize readership I'd like to place your ad beside this editorial. Is that alright or would you prefer a different position?*

In each of these examples the prospect places the order by selecting one of the two choices.

**Steps to success**
To familiarize yourself with closing techniques write out another 10 examples of the Alternative Choice Close.

# The Stall Close

Unfortunately, when we ask our prospects to make a choice they sometimes respond by saying *"I'm not sure about that so I'll get back to you."* The Stall Close is a powerful technique that allows you to book the schedule when your prospect is having difficulty making a decision, because the Stall Close circumvents the prospect's indecisiveness.

For example, you've tried to close the prospect by saying *Ms. Prospect, I've reserved your ad in the August issue. Did you want Reader Service information requests sent to your attention or to someone else?* But instead of making a choice, she says *"I'm not quite sure about that. Let me think it over and I'll get back to you."*

Using the Stall Close you would respond by saying, *Ms. Prospect, that's okay. I really don't need to know that right now. I'll immediately reserve your space in the August issue and you can let me know about the Reader Service information requests later.*

Here's another example. You've asked a closing question but the prospect stalls by saying, *"I haven't decided whether to run this as a 2 color or full color ad, so let me think it over and I'll get back to you."* Keeping in mind that most prospects who say *"I'll get back to you"* never do, your best chance of booking the ad is now.

*Mr. Prospect, that's okay. I really don't need to know that right now. I'll immediately reserve your space in the August issue and you can let me know about the color next week.*

When using the Stall Close the pattern is always the same.

*I really don't need to know that right now. I'll immediately reserve your space and you can let me know about that later.*

# The Minor Point Close

The Minor Point Close is similar to the Alternative Choice close but instead of asking the prospect to choose between two minor points, the closing question is phrased, so that a yes or a no response leads to a sale.

*Mr. Prospect, the artwork for your ad will be ready for review next Thursday. Is that soon enough?*

*Mr. Prospect, I'll send a copy of the magazine, containing your ad to your office each month. Should I send it to your attention?*

*Mr. Prospect, I have booked your ad in the June issue which includes a complimentary ad in the Buyer's Guide. Did you want to take advantage of this free listing?*

*Mr. Prospect, to maximize readership I'd like to place your ad beside this editorial. Is that position all right?*

*Mr. Prospect, I have reserved your ½ page ad in the October issue. Will you be sending us the artwork by email?*

*Mr. Prospect, reader response is tracked and the leads will be sent to your attention. Should I send them to this email address?*

# The One Good Reason Close

At the end of your presentation simply ask the prospect if he can think of one good reason why he shouldn't book the campaign today. If he can't think of a reason he has agreed to buying, if he can, he's limited himself to one reason.

When using this technique, always remind the prospect of the reason for booking today.

*Mr. Prospect, can you think of one good reason why you wouldn't want to guarantee your place in the December issue by reserving your space today?*

*Ms Prospect, can you think of one good reason why you wouldn't want to increase your sales and profits by offering your services to over 15,000 perspective customers?*

*Mr. Prospect, can you think of one good reason why you wouldn't take advantage of the free upgrade by giving us the go-ahead today?*

# The Feel, Felt, Found Close

This is a universal closing technique that can be used to handle a multitude of different situations.

**I don't think this will work for me**
*Mr. Prospect, I understand how you* ***feel*** *and many of my clients* ***felt*** *the same way. But after running an ad in our publication they* ***found*** *that the resulting sales and leads, far outweighed their investment. Isn't that what you are looking for?*

**This is too expensive**
*Mr. Prospect, I understand how you* ***feel*** *and many of our repeat customers originally* ***felt*** *the same way. But after running an ad in our publication they* ***found*** *that the resulting sales and profits, far outweighed their investment. Isn't that what you are looking for?*

# The Direct Close

The Direct Close has been left for last, because it is the weakest of all closing techniques, yet it is still far better to use the Direct Close than not to close at all. If you keep in mind that you should only ask a closing question when you know that your prospect is ready to order, the odds of landing the account are in your favor.

If you've made a powerful presentation that solved your prospect's marketing problem, your prospect already recognizes the value in using your services, so just ask for the order.

*Mr. Prospect, can I reserve your ad in the May issue?*

*Mr. Prospect, would you like to go-ahead with this campaign?*

If he says *"No"* don't give up. Instead, ask him why. *"Mr. Prospect, I believe this campaign will bring great results and I thought you felt the same way, yet you seem hesitant. May I ask why?"*

This question will draw out his concerns; address these concerns and close again.

# Using the Conditional Close to deal with procrastination

The premise of this technique is to close the sale, conditional upon the prospect's right to cancel. When using the Conditional Close always give your prospect a reason to order today.

**I'd like to think it over**
*Mr. Prospect, I understand there is a lot to think about, but to prevent someone else from taking your space I'll reserve it immediately. In the meantime you can think it over and if for any reason you decide to change your mind just let me know next week and I'll cancel. It's a simple way of protecting your interests. Isn't that a good idea?*

**I haven't decided whether to go with a ½ page or a ¼ page**
*Mr. Prospect, I understand, but ad space for the June issue is selling out quickly, so I'll reserve your ½ page immediately. In the meantime you can think it over and if you decide to go with a ¼ page instead, just let me know next week and I'll make the adjustment. It's a simple way of protecting your interests. Isn't that a good idea?*

**I'd still like to look at another publication before I decide**

*Mr. Prospect, I understand because most of my clients did exactly the same thing. But space for the August issue is selling out quickly so I'll reserve your space immediately. In the meantime you can compare publications and should you decide to change your mind just let me know next week and I'll cancel. It's a simple way of protecting your interests. Isn't that a good idea?*

**I want to run this by my advertising agency first**

*Mr. Prospect, I understand because many of my clients have the same policy. But space for the August issue is selling out quickly so I'll reserve your space immediately. In the meantime you can discuss this with your ad agency and should you decide to change your mind just let me know next week and I'll cancel. It's a simple way of protecting your interests. Isn't that a good idea?*

# The Next Appointment Close

Irrespective of how hard you try some prospects will simply refuse to see the logic of giving you the go-ahead today.

The premise of the Next Appointment Close is to put yourself in position for a future close by setting a specific time and date for the next meeting. But the Next Appointment Close is a response of last resort, so use it only after you've tried all the other techniques. Here's what to say.

*Mr. Prospect, I understand, so why don't we touch base next week to see how you made out and I can answer any questions that may have arisen.*

IMPORTANT: Don't say *"Why don't we meet next..."* be sure to use the words *"touch base."*

Now wait for the prospect to say *"Okay"* and then closing for the appointment.

*Great, I can be at your office Monday morning at 9:00 or do you prefer 10:30?*

# Helping your clients with expert advice

# Guru at work

If you had a plumbing problem which of the following would you call for advice; an accountant, a carpenter or a plumber? If your car was overheating, who would be best suited to fix the problem: a lawyer, a gardener or an auto mechanic? If you were interested in direct mail, who would you contact: a printer, a graphic artist or a direct mail specialist?

In almost every case people prefer to deal with a specialist and your prospects are no different. They want to work with someone they can rely on, who can make suggestions and offer ideas; preferably an expert in the field and they'll gladly pay a premium to anyone who can increase their probability of success and reduce their risk of failure.

Without question, positioning yourself as a marketing expert is a powerful technique that will result in an instant increase in sales and reduce the need to prospect. While most salespeople are burdened with the task of continually seeking-out new clients, clients are desperately searching for experts that can solve their marketing problems.

*"This sounds like a good idea except for one small problem - I'm no marketing expert"* This is the response I usually get when I tell salespeople to offer expert advice, because most salespeople underestimate their expertise. For example,

Could you show your prospects how to gain market share?
Could you make recommendations that would make their ad campaign more effective?
Could you show them how to increase sales and generate leads?
Could you advise them on ad size, color and positioning?
Could you share ideas about your market?
Could you show your prospects how to reduce their marketing cost?
Are you already helping your clients solve their marketing problems?

The answer to all of the above is *"Yes"* because you are already an expert and to further your expertise here are the techniques that top ad agencies use to create powerful ads that sell. Share some of these ideas with your prospects and you'll instantly transform yourself from a salesperson to a marketing guru.

# How magazine ads are read

To better understand how magazine adverting works let's follow Jack, the owner of a retail store as he reads a copy of Best Retail Magazine.

The first thing Jack will do is flip through the pages and as he does he'll get exposed to dozens of ads and articles all vying for his attention. Now Jack won't stop at each and every ad to see if it has something of value to offer, instead he'll only give an ad an idle glance as he quickly scans each page. In that split second, Jack must, and I stress must, see or sense some reason to pause and Jack will only pause if he sees or senses some benefit for pausing.

During that split second, as Jack scans each page his eyes will be drawn to illustrations and photographs first, so here is your client's first and possibly only opportunity to grab the reader's attention.

If Jack stopped at the illustration, the next thing he'll do is quickly scan, not read, the headline and if he feels that the headline offers a probable benefit only then will he consider reading the rest of the copy.

# Expert advice on photography and illustrations

1. **Does the ad include a photo or illustration?**
   *Mr. Prospect, have you considered adding a photograph or illustration to your ad. These have extremely high readership and are known to increase response.*

2. **Is the photo or illustration instantly recognizable?**
   That's not to say that your clients shouldn't be creative, they should, as long as it does not detract from quick and easy understanding.
   *Mr. Prospect, the reader will decide whether or not to pause at your ad within a millisecond, so the photo or illustration must be instantly recognizable or the reader will pass it by.*

3. **Does the illustration make a contribution to the ad?**
   Always ensure that your client's illustration is used to communicate a benefit.
   *Mrs. Prospect, if the illustration does not make a significant contribution to the ad you are not taking full advantage of the advertising space so you might want to consider using a strong headline instead.*

4. **Does the ad promote a number of different products?**
To prevent confusion and to keep the reader focused, the ad should promote one product or idea.
*Mr. Prospect, I notice that your photograph contains a number of different images. Tests have shown that ads that focus on one product or idea get the highest response.*

5. **Does the ad include a caption?**
More people read captions then read body copy so always include a caption or headline under the illustration.
*Ms Prospect, may I suggest that you place a caption* <u>*under*</u> *your illustration. Captions have extremely high readership and can be used to pull the reader into your copy.*

6. **Does the ad show the equipment or machinery in use?**
*Mr. Prospect, equipment and machinery often look dull when not in use. Have you considered giving your ad action by showing the product being used? To create the illusion of movement you could;*
   - *use a series of images showing the equipment in action, or*
   - *create a blurred effect by having the camera or subject move.*

7. **Does the ad include people?**
   *Mr. Prospect, on average, illustrations that include people are twice as effective at attracting attention as those without so you might want to consider adding people to your photo.*

8. **Keep the background simple**
   *Mr. Prospect, which do you want the reader to notice, your product or the interesting background? If you want them to focus on your product don't give them the choice, so keep the background simple.*

# Expert advice on headlines

*Mr. Prospect, industry experts agree that the headline accounts for 90% of the success of the ad, because if the reader doesn't like the headline he won't read the rest of your copy, so may I suggest that you place a strong headline at the top of your copy.*

*Ms Prospect, although the headline can be as creative as its author, there are 3 types of headlines that consistently score highest on the readership scale; headlines that offer a benefit; headlines that offer practical advice and headlines that offer new information.*

**Headlines that offer a benefit**
Read your client's headline; does it offer a benefit or a feature? Features describe the product or service while benefits tell the reader what the product or service will do for them.
*Mrs. Prospect, I notice that your headline offers a feature. Tests have shown that headlines that tell the reader how he will benefit from using the product generate the highest response.*

**Headlines that offer practical advice**
*Mr. Prospect, one of the best ways to attract readers is to offer practical advice because people find it difficult to by-pass headlines that show them how to reach their goals.*

**Headlines that offer new information**
*Mr. Prospect, is your ad announcing a new product; an improvement in an old product or a new way to use an existing product? The reason I ask is that people that read trade magazines often scan these publications looking for new products and information, so writing a headline that satisfies their interest will stop them at your ad.*

Here's some expert advice that will ensure that your client's headline gets attention.

1. **Is your client using a Blind headline?**
   *Mr. Prospect, I notice that you're using a Blind headline; in other words it doesn't tell the reader what the product is or what it will do. Blind headlines are least effective because the reader must look to the body copy for an explanation, but often he won't get that far.*

2. **Does the headline use precise figures?**
   For example, instead of writing "Ours is the best selling product" your client could write "Over 11,000 sold last year"
   *Mr. Prospect, to make your headline stronger and more believable, consider using precise figures instead of generalities.*

3. **How long should the headline be?**
   *Ms Prospect, a number of leading experts claim that a headline should be limited to a maximum of seven words but other studies have shown that long headlines are often more effective then short headlines. So when writing your headline the best rule to follow is this; keep your words*

*to a minimum but use as many words as you need, because it's not the number of words in the headline that determines readership but rather your message.*

4. **Is the client using a long headline?**
*Mr. Prospect, to make your long headline easy to read, may I suggest that you break and stack it into visual gulps. But don't use more than 3 visual gulps.*

5. **Is the headline easy to read?**
*Mr. Prospect, say it in your headline in the same way that you would say it in everyday conversation, so don't use stilted language or clichés.*

6. **Which decision maker is your client trying to reach?**
*Mr. Prospect, although the headline should stress the strongest possible benefit to the largest number of people, always write your headline with an individual prospect in mind. For example, if your ad is directed at the owner, ensure that your headline focuses on the owner's interests and talk the owner's language.*

7. **Does the headline standout?**
*Mr. Prospect, the headline is the most important part of your ad, so may I suggest that you set it large and in bold so that it stands out.*

# Expert advice on body copy

*Ms Prospect, the most important part of your ad, next to the illustration and headline is the lead-in sentence because the reader will often use the lead-in sentence to decide whether or not the rest of your ad is worth reading.*

1. **Is the ad lighthearted or humorous?**
*Mr. Prospect, although humorous or lighthearted ads may get attention, they usually don't get a high response, so may I suggest that you keep the tone of your ad serious and give your readers the facts.*

2. **Does the ad get to the point quickly?**
*Mr. Prospect, although your prospects will read long copy, they will not spend time guessing what your ad is all about so get-to-the-point-copy gets the highest readership.*

3. **Has the ad been written with an individual in mind?**
*Mr. Prospect, is your ad directed at the owner, general manager or production manager? The reason I ask is each of these decision makers has different interests so you must write your copy with a specific person in mind.*

4. **Does the ad give complete information?**
*Mrs. Prospect, readers often clip and file ads for future reference, so unless you are designing a lead generating ad that asks the reader to request a free catalogue or brochure, don't leave the reader*

*guessing as to what your product or service can and cannot do.*

5. **Does the ad offer to solve a problem?**
   *Mr. Prospect, instead of designing an ad that describes your product or service show the reader how your product or service will solve their problem and you'll get a higher response.*

6. **Is the copy too long?**
   *Mr. Prospect, don't be concerned about the length of the copy. As long as it keeps the reader interested it will get read.*

7. **Is the copy easy to understand?**
   *Mr. Prospect, don't use a magazine ad to showcase linguistic skills. If the reader can't instantly understand what you are saying, they'll stop reading.*

8. **Is the headline repeated at the end of copy?**
   *Mr. Prospect, repeating the headline is an effective direct mail copy writing technique because the prospect is often encouraged to read several pages of copy but it is usually a waste of words when used in a magazine ad.*

9. **Does the ad tell the reader what action to take next?**
   *Ms Prospect, ads that give the reader clear instructions on what action to take next are twice as effective as those which leave the reader to draw his own conclusions. So your ad should give the reader a reason to act immediately.*

# Expert advice on formatting

For the reader to follow the ad, his eyes must enter and exit the ad where they should, and research shows that we read pages from upper left corner to the lower right corner, in a series of horizontal sweeps, always moving down from where we start. This pattern is called reading gravity.

1. **Is the flow of the ad difficult to follow?**
   *Mr. Prospect, one way to defy reading gravity is to number the sections in the order that you want the prospect to read them.*

2. **Is the benefit or illustration positioned in the top half of the page?**
   *Mrs. Prospect, a reader could, with a glance at the upper left quarter of the page, not even see the rest of the ad because going from that quarter to the lower right quarter demands movement of the head, not just the pupils. So ensure that the most important benefits get noticed by placing them at the top of the ad.*

3. **Is the headline positioned above the illustration?**
   *Mr. Prospect, the reader's eyes go to the picture first and then travel down the page, so any copy placed above the illustration may be missed.*

4. **Is the headline and illustration together?**
   *Mr. Prospect, an illustration, immediately followed by a strong headline has the highest readership.*

5. **Are subheadings being used to break-up long copy and to stress major points?**
   *Mr. Prospect, the reader will often scan your ad before reading the copy so subheadings offer a great opportunity to grab the reader's attention and encourage him to read on.*

6. **Are the paragraphs short?**
   *Mr. Prospect, studies have consistently shown that long paragraphs don't get read, so keep your paragraphs short.*

7. **When selecting a typeface the primary consideration must be easy readability.**
   The easier the ad is to read the more likely it will be read. So here's a short guide to the most readable typeface and settings.

   a. Use a typeface with rounded serif – which means no sans serif
   b. Use faces with short to medium length ascenders and decenders
   c. Set headlines in bold, set copy in regular, 11 pt body copy is ideal
   d. Bold copy should never be smaller than 9 pt and use 10 – 14 pt if space permits
   e. An upper and lower case headline beats an all upper case headline in readability because words set in upper and lower case form a distinctive shape the reader can easily recognize
   f. Don't try to gain advertising space by reducing line spacing. Narrow line spacing hinders readership

g. To make the ad easy to read, use black print on a white background or at the very least dark letters on a pale background.
h. As a general rule the ad should have no more than two different kinds of typeface
i. Use reverse type for headlines and very short copy only and even then the background must be solid. So avoid using reverse over a photographic background.

# Expert advice on positioning, color, frequency, circulation and size

## Color

*Mr. Prospect, studies have shown the addition of just one color can increase readership by over 20% and that a four-color ad will draw between 30 – 50% higher readership than a black and white ad. Plus adding color,*

- *enhances your credibility and*
- *can increase the impact of what you want to say by drawing the reader's attention to colored phrase and words.*

## Size

*Mrs. Prospect, as a general rule the larger the ad, the higher the readership. But this does not mean that you must run a full-page ad, but rather that your ad must be large enough to standout.*

*Mr. Prospect, studies have shown that readers associate the size of the ad with the size of the company; small ad – small company; large ad – big business.*

## Positioning

*Mr. Prospect, ads printed on the inside cover; on page one; opposite the table of contents and on the back cover get the highest readership.*

*Mr. Prospect, in consumer magazines, ads that appear in the first 10% of the publication get higher readership, but this rule does not hold true for trade publications with strong editorial content. The reader of a trade magazine is looking for information and a well written, informative editorial will pull him through the entire publication.*

*Mr. Prospect, if the magazine has excellent editorial content, then your ad will do well in the front, middle or back of the publication. If the magazine has weak editorial content, be sure to place your ad in the front 10%.*

*Mr. Prospect, ads placed on the right side are slightly more visible and arguably have higher readership, but an attention getting article placed on the right hand side will increase readership to ads on the opposite page.*

*Mr. Prospect, unless you're purchasing premium ad space, editorial content is of paramount importance, because it has a direct effect on readership; high quality editorials mean higher readership which translates into higher response.*

## Frequency

*Mr. Prospect, although a well written ad can generate instant response, studies have shown that your message must penetrate the mind of the prospect a total of 6 times before the prospect becomes a customer, so frequency is an important part of your advertising campaign.*

## Circulation

*Mr. Prospect, not to suggest that circulation is unimportant but rather there is no relationship between circulation and response because response is the result of readership not circulation and readership is directly proportional to editorial content.*

*Mr. Prospect, when selecting a publication don't base your decision on circulation. Always weigh circulation against editorial content and you'll usually find that the publication with the best editorial content will bring you the highest return.*

*About the Author*

**Peter Ebner** is a professional sales trainer and marketing consultant with over 25 years of experience. He is author of 12 books and audio programs including the best seller *Breaking the Print Sales Barrier*. He lectures throughout North America, South America, Europe and South Africa.

To contact the author or learn about upcoming seminars email us at peter@SellingMagazineAds.com or call (905) 713-2274

www.SellingMagazineAds.com